Leaving a Legacy of Love

Lessons from Ruth and Boaz

Their Love, Redemption, Leadership, and Legacy

Leonard P. Cole

Scripture taken from the King James Version of the Bible.

Cole Legacy Publisher books may be ordered through Amazon.com.

Cole Legacy Publishers

Temecula, California

ISBN 9798358983410

Library of Congress Control Number: 2015916991

CONTENTS

INTRODUCTION

Marrying at the early age of eighteen had its challenges for my wife, Lynn, and me. Our first challenge was to find a place for her to stay while I shipped out overseas. We were on a budget and only had a couple of days to get her a place to live. My plan was to find her something clean and convenient. We finally found a small unit behind a widow's house. I thought it was a perfect place for my wife. Without listening to her, I went ahead and rented the unit. Shortly after I left for overseas, it became apparent that she was too isolated living in this small backyard house. She was lonely and needed to be in proximity of people she knew. This house was out of our neighborhood. I was not sensitive to her feelings. She ended up moving in with friends after two days. When she wrote me and gave me the news of her moving out of the house, I was convicted that I had lacked leadership in my decision. I had not taken her thoughts and feelings into consideration. This was the beginning of many learning experiences for me.

Studying Ruth helped define my life and the values I later placed on marriage and family. I learned about the role men are assigned in honoring, protecting, and providing for women. Later, I gleaned management and leadership principles through reading and studying Boaz's actions.

The book of Ruth is responsible for my being able to experience a richer marriage during each year for over sixty years. I read the book many times when I had to make decisions or contemplated how to respond to my wife. For her part, she consulted several books in the Bible trying to figure out how to respond to me.

Boaz sets the example for how men should lead their families. He waited many years to get married, and during that time, the Lord refined him into a wonderful husband, father, and leader. Boaz no doubt received instruction from his parents.

I received some guidance from my parents, but found a wealth of instruction from Sunday school, church attendance, and Bible study. I started attending Sunday school when I was a toddler. I can remember attending Sunday school at the age of three at the old Missionary Baptist Church in San Pedro, California. A sweet, elderly woman, Mrs. Thomas, was my teacher. She held a big

Bible with her two hands and told us stories about a powerful God.

A couple of years later, we moved to another town, and my father made sure my older brother, Jim, and I went to church. He either dropped us off or told us to ride our bicycles. Every Sunday morning, I heard Bible stories and followed along in my own Bible.

One Sunday morning, as I sat in a chair, alternating between staring out the window and looking at the easel in front of me, I was prompted to answer a question. Mrs. Northrop, the pastor's wife, walked over to the easel and placed a cut-out figure of a woman dressed in purple.

"This is Ruth, the Moabite widow, and Naomi's daughter-in-law. Do any of you know about Ruth?"

My hand shot up. "I have an aunt named Ruth."

All the boys and girls laughed. I was seven years old, and this was junior church. In Sunday school, we were learning the books of the Old Testament, so I was familiar with Ruth and where to find it. But I only thought it was about my aunt Ruth.

Later in her storytelling, Mrs. Northrop put up a figure of an important-looking man and told us about Boaz. As she continued telling us the story of Ruth and Boaz and their marriage, my thoughts drifted—I wanted to be rich and own a large ranch. I was not interested in marriage, because at age seven, I was convinced you had to sit and wait too long while a woman put on her makeup and jewelry and figured out which pair of shoes to wear.

Several grades later, the story made a lot of sense to me. The attributes of love, redemption, leadership, and legacy came true to me as the years progressed. The more I read about Boaz and how he served the Lord, the more I wanted to emulate him.

Because I married young, I only had a basic understanding of what was expected of me. My nineteen-year-old wife, Lynn, was patient with me as I grew in knowledge. Thankfully, I studied the book of Ruth and discovered many concepts that helped me to become a better husband, spiritual leader, and father. Ruth and Boaz give us a beautiful love story. Their story provides a foundation for how a good marriage can become better. The central theme of this book is strengthening marriages and passing core values to the generations that follow you.

This is not a scholarly book. It takes the truth of Scripture and applies it to the four dimensions that are important in marriage. These four dimensions are love, leadership, redemption, and legacy.

It contrasts principles expressed in Ruth with current cultural values. Insights on present-day men and their condition when it comes to courting, marriage, and responsibility are discussed. It is my hope that you will enjoy reading this story and come away with a greater understanding of God's sovereignty, providence, and grace to us all.

The book of Ruth was written around 1000 B.C. The events described in the Scriptures occurred around 1,300 B.C. to 1,200 B.C. The author is unknown but may have been Samuel. The story occurred during a turbulent period when the Judges governed Israel (1380 B.C. to 1050 B.C.) During this time, God's people practiced idolatry and were unfaithful to Him.

This love story takes place during a dark time for Israel. The story begins with a famine in Bethlehem and ends with a return to prosperity in that region. Ruth shows God's grace. He gave a non-Jewish person, Ruth, a place in the genealogy of David (Ruth 4:17) and Christ (Matthew 1:5).This small Old Testament book reveals much about the character of God and His sovereignty. It tells us about Ruth and Boaz diligently following the providence of our Lord.

The objective of this book is to make good marriages better and to help married couples experience the importance of passing on a legacy of a good marriage and family to their descendants. It is my purpose to equip men for their leadership responsibilities in the home.

Soli Deo gloria!

To God alone be the glory!

CHAPTER 1

You Can't Just Live on Love

> Now it came to pass in the days when the judges ruled, that there was a famine in the land. And a certain man of Bethlehem-judah, went to sojurn in the country of Moab, he, and his wife, and his two sons. And the name of the man was Elimelech, the name of his wife was Naomi, and the names of his two sons were Mahlon and Chilion, Ephrathites of Bethlehem-judah. And they came into the country of Moab, and continued there.
>
> —Ruth 1:1–2

During my time serving in the army, my wife, Lynn, and I lived on Okinawa. This was June 1963 through July 1965. I was paid once per month, and we lived on a monthly budget of $155. On payday, I bought a money order and mailed the difference between my pay and the $155 to our bank in the States. Lynn and I then placed money in envelopes. We budgeted $40 for food,

$6 for entertainment, $85 for rent, $20 for electricity, and the remaining $4 for incidentals, including bus fare.

Oftentimes, near the end of the month, we found ourselves searching for pennies, nickels, and dimes. We hoped to find enough to ride the bus to the army post. It was three cents each way per person. If we wanted to see a movie, it cost fifteen cents per person. A bag of popcorn cost ten cents. If we could find fifty-two cents, it was a go. I remember one night we found forty cents and decided to walk a couple of miles in the sweltering heat and humidity to go to the movies.

One month, we missed planning for meals by a day. We got up the morning before payday without any food in the house. We knew a couple of days ahead of time that our cupboards would be empty. My wife did not complain. Lynn found some flour and fashioned it into pie crust. She sprinkled it with cinnamon, baked it, and served it to me with a smile. I worked the day shift at that time and walked to the army post. It was in the heat of the summer. On Okinawa, you will sweat at five in the morning, even if you are standing doing nothing. By the time I reached the post, I was drenched with sweat. When I got down to the compound where I worked, I went into the restroom and splashed water on my face. I drank a generous portion of water. I ate nothing for lunch, as my separate-rations status required I pay twenty-four cents for lunch.

That night, I walked home, and Lynn greeted me with a hug and kiss and brought out the near-empty pie plate. There were still some crumbs left over. We sat in the kitchen and talked about our dinner dates back home and how we used to go for a hamburger and malt. I worked rotating shifts, and payday was my day off this month. I was required to go up to the post and report for my pay. Lynn insisted I get a hamburger first and then come and get her; we would go back up to the post together and have a decent meal at the café. Then we would take a bus down island to the post exchange for our month's supply of groceries. We executed the plan and experienced a wonderful day going down island to stock up with food.

Fortunately for us, it was only a day and a half with no food. When we read in the book of Ruth about the famine in Bethlehem, we realized there were probably many days without food for its inhabitants. Elimelech and his family were destitute. He knew he had to do something.

I could imagine one distant morning at sunrise and Elimelech looking out the window and seeing the wind kicking up dust around the property. It had not rained in months. He most likely wondered how to feed his family that day.

One could visualize the scene with Naomi, his wife, waking up to the neighbor's soon-to-be-eaten goats bleating in the distance. She looked at Elimelech. "Good morning, my love," she said as she gave him a hug and a kiss. "I will fetch some water." She looked toward the nearly dry well.

Even though Bethlehem means "house of bread," it did not help them. Elimelech, whose name means "God is King," believed it was time to move somewhere else. There was no food and no means to produce any.

This is our home—it will be a hard decision to leave our land, he thought as he looked outside and took in their parched property with his sleepy eyes. *But I must move to where I can provide for my family.*

Elimelech gazed out the window and saw Naomi bringing up a sparse amount of water. Naomi brought the water into the house and smiled as she poured Elimelech a portion for him to drink. His throat was parched, and as the water trickled down to his empty stomach, he thought, *Now is the time to talk to Naomi*.

He stood up. "We need to talk. I have been thinking about us moving to Moab. A man at the gate said there is plenty of food there and an opportunity for me to get work. It will be a difficult move, but we have no other option since we are out of food."

Naomi welled up with emotion, looked around, and then whispered, "So be it."

Elimelech then told their teenage boys, Mahlon and Chilion, to start packing their belongings. Mahlon means "sickly" and Chilion means "failing."

The next morning, the family of four packed up their essential belongings and headed toward Moab. Elimelech and Naomi stood together and surveyed the home and property they were about to abandon. "Well, let's get going," a dejected Elimelech said as they started walking. The sun was rising, and cocks were crowing. It was important that they get a start toward Moab before the sun flamed overhead. It would take them several days to get there. They were all hungry, and there was no place to stop for food before they started out. They planned to barter some of their belongings for food once they left Bethlehem.

As they walked down the road, the dust whipped up and smacked them in the face. It was approximately fifty unpleasant miles to Moab, with the trip traversing some rough terrain. (Moab is in modern-day Jordan.)

There is no indication that Elimelech sought out the Lord's guidance on whether to move from Bethlehem to a strange land or stay put until the famine ended. In God's providence, He orchestrates events for His purposes. As we will later see, God used this situation to fulfill His purposes through Elimelech's decision to go to a strange land.

I worked long hours in our compound at the army post. It was a small post with all four branches of the service and two civilian government agencies. I was embedded with the National Security Agency (NSA). For several months, we were understaffed. I worked fourteen-hour days with no break. To make matters worse, we experienced a drought on the island. Usually the water was on during my shift. Therefore, I could not take a shower. When Lynn came to the island, I had her fill up a pail and a canteen with water while I was at work. We used the pail of water to flush the toilet and the canteen for me to take a sticky sponge bath. It was a miserable time, but I knew it would eventually end and continued to work hard.

We finally received relief soldiers from the States and went back to eight-hour days. I decided to increase my income with a part-time job. Several nights a week, when I was not working the swing shift, I worked as a janitor. It paid eighty dollars per month, tax-free. This gave us a buffer in case we ran out of money. I still adhered to our budget, but I staggered the money I sent to our savings account. We gave to the base chapel and missionaries down island whenever we could. We had to use soldiers with a top-secret critical intelligence clearance to keep our compound clean, so this was a steady part-time job.

One night, when I came home after finishing my janitor job, I found out my wife had purchased furniture with the extra money. I think she decided that since she was the keeper of the home, she had the authority to make the decision to purchase the furniture. It was bright persimmon Naugahyde vinyl, and it added color to our home. I was glad we had some wiggle room and could adjust our budget. We were still sorting out marriage, budgeting, and joint decision making. My priority was to have enough money to cover our living expenses. She wanted to replace some broken-down furniture and add color to our house.

As the months went by, it became apparent that my budgeting was too tight. I limited our fun by not allowing enough money and time for recreation. We had no phone and no transportation. Since Lynn was the chaplain's volunteer secretary, she asked him to come speak to me. He came to our house one evening when I was not working and had a man-to-man talk with me. Here I was, a private first class, receiving instruction from an army captain. The chaplain told me to take a leave and spend some money on my wife. I was humbled. In my quest to be the ultimate provider, I had selfishly only considered my feelings and not my wife's. I asked Lynn where she wanted to go, and she said she wanted to go to the main Japanese island of Honshu.

We decided to make it an adventure and booked a cabin on a Japanese freighter headed for Honshu. We were on the top level with a private room. The next level down was a large, open area packed with people. All other levels held cattle. The captain's chef charged the high price of a dollar each for breakfast the first day out. He moistened our griddled toast with fish oil. I did not order breakfast again. I get seasick anyway.

The freighter stopped at two small scenic islands during our two-day cruise. We got off the ship at the second island. The inhabitants supported themselves by selling belts and wallets made out of snake skin. They had an abundance of snakes, and it provided revenue for them.

We arrived at Honshu and docked at Kobe. Lynn and I were excited to get off the ship and explore the town. We checked into a traditional Japanese hotel. Our room was covered with mats and a floor bed. I was eager to take a hot shower or tub soak. It had been a long time since I had been able to enjoy either. I took a long tub soak and enjoyed the refreshing hot water. We went out that night and found a Japanese coffee house. In English, the sign said "coffee music." It had coffee, music, and ice cream. The people who worked there welcomed us and made sure we had a pleasant visit.

The next day, we took a train to Tokyo and toured the city for two days. This trip revitalized our marriage and gave me time to relax after several months of stressful long work hours. We decided to fly back rather than take the freighter. I had enough money for Lynn to fly back, but not enough for me. I purchased a ticket for her and asked the clerk at the counter if I could pay mine later. After consultation with management, the clerk agreed to give me a ticket and held my army duffle bag hostage until I paid. I figured I had enough uniforms at home and could do without it for a couple of weeks. We boarded the plane and headed to Naha, Okinawa. Two weeks later, when I got paid, I went down island, gave the airline the eighty-five dollars I owed them, and picked up my duffle bag. During our vacation, I received a promotion to specialist E-4 with a pay raise.

We finally purchased an old, banged-up motor scooter for transportation. It ran well and gave us the freedom we needed to explore the island and have fun. When payday came along, we took the scooter down island to purchase our groceries. One day, we purchased fourteen bags of groceries and somehow managed to pack all of them on the scooter. We must have looked funny riding down the highway. The only problem we experienced was that a cloudburst soaked the groceries and us. Fortunately, we got home without losing anything and dried out our purchases. The scooter helped our marriage. It allowed us to explore and enjoy the island.

We adopted a dog, a cocker spaniel, and he lived in the house with us. One night, he started throwing up. We decided Lynn would take him on a bus down island to the veterinarian the next morning while I went to my job at the post. She boarded the bus full of people. The driver permitted all kinds of animals. As the bus headed down the highway, the dog began to throw up. Lynn instinctively stuck his head out the window. A man behind her was reading a newspaper, and fortunately, only the front page of his newspaper got splattered as the wind wafted the vomit back into the bus through his window. The vet's diagnosis was distemper. Lynn had to leave the dog with him. We had another dog that came with our rented house. His name was Phillip. He sat on our porch most of the time. We never let him in the house and never fed him. Neighbors complained to us about Phillip leaving messes around the housing complex. We could do nothing since he roamed free and belonged to the house, not us. Phillip was immune to everything and never got sick.

These first two years of our marriage helped us to sort our many things. We had no family around to help or interfere and little money. It was just us. We belonged to a Bible study group that met once a week. Sometimes I could not attend the study, since I worked rotating shifts. A missionary couple who focused on reaching out to military personnel hosted it. We still keep in contact with this couple today. One of the lessons I learned during these early years is that when you have nothing but each other, you can build a rich relationship when you include the Lord. We focused on sorting out our marriage issues and grew in the Lord.

CHAPTER 2

Losing the Love of Your Life

> Then Elimelech, Naomi's husband, died; and she was left, and her two sons. Now they took wives of the women of Moab: the name of the one was Orpah and the name of the other Ruth. And they dwelt there about ten years. Then both Mahlon and Chilion also died; so the woman survived her two sons and her husband. (Ruth 1:3–5)

During this time, the Israelites were under the ten-generation prohibition from allowing the male offspring of a mixed marriage with a Moabite into their congregation. There was no prohibition on men marrying Moabite women. The Moabites descended from Lot as a result of his incestuous relation with his older daughter. The Moabites evidently were not enemies of Israel during this time, as Elimelech and his family were freely accepted in the land.

Elimelech took a great risk bringing his family to Moab. In Psalm 108:9, God said that Moab is His washpot. This is a way of saying that Moab is disgusting. The land and its inhabitants were less than desirable and not respected by the Israelites. Elimelech risked his family being corrupted by the idolatry and other pagan influences in the land.

The boys married Moabite women but fathered no children.

Elimelech died and left Naomi a widow. Naomi, whose name means "pleasant," still had her two sons and Moabite daughters-in-law, but not for long. As Naomi was still grieving the loss of Elimelech, her two sons, Mahlon and Chilion, died, possibly due to failing health. It is tragic to lose one's spouse, but then to lose your children shortly thereafter is beyond comprehension. This was too much for Naomi.

Naomi was left with two widowed daughters-in-law. She believed God was punishing her. She was in a strange land with no means of support. God had a plan for her, but she just didn't know it yet.

> Then she arose with her daughters-in-law, that she might return from the country of Moab: for she had heard in the country of Moab how that

> the Lord had visited his people in giving them bread. (Ruth 1:6)

In this passage, Naomi was standing on the road to Bethlehem, wondering what to do next. She did not fully understand what had happened to her. It would take some time before she realized what was going on behind the scenes. God was orchestrating something on her behalf that would unfold before her in a beautiful way. She was under God's providential care. When our biblical account continues, Naomi heard in town that Israel's famine was over. Now she was ready to go home to the land of Judah. She longed to return to her birthplace. This next passage takes place at a crossroad.

Imagine a marker that says Bethlehem 50 Miles and another that says Moab Town Limits, pointing in the opposite direction. It was getting hot and the wind was howling as Naomi exhorted her daughters-in-law to stay and let her go home by herself.

Recently, an elderly widow came into my office to get her taxes prepared. She normally gave to her church, and I asked her how much she gave last year. She said she had given nothing and did not attend church anymore, because a god who had taken away her husband did not deserve her worship and money. She further told me she harbored resentment and anger toward God. She and her husband had enjoyed many good years of retirement activity together, and she greatly missed him. Like so many people, she did not comprehend the sovereignty of God. She blamed God for her loss.

This is a natural reaction. Her husband of more than sixty years was gone, and she did not understand why God had taken him. A lack of spiritual preparation for this loss took its toll on her. Naomi's condition matched this woman's. Naomi ignored the character of God by calling herself bitter. Naomi experienced difficulty since she had lost all the males in her household and the financial support and companionship they had brought her. Her tragic loss created emotional discouragement for her as she tried to confront the reality of it. In God's plan and sovereignty, the eventual result was a blessing for Naomi.

A navy chaplain who had served during the Korean War told me an interesting story about people confronting the deaths of family members. After he'd served a tour in Korea during the war, the military sent him to the

States as a casualty chaplain. His job required him to visit families of sailors killed in the line of duty and tell them of the sailors' deaths. He said Bible-believing Christian families understood the sovereignty of God and thereby understood that God was in control. For him, the most difficult family members to work with were those with no belief in God. They exhibited no understanding of eternal purposes, and to them, nothing occurred beyond death. They could not be comforted.

Another of my widowed clients, who lost her husband a couple of years ago, misses him but is willing to acknowledge God's timing for him to go home. She did not know, but five years previously, he had come to my office alone. His thirty-year career as military pilot had taken him to Vietnam, where he had contracted cancer from Agent Orange. He knew his days were numbered and wanted to make the most of them, but he also wanted to financially care for his wife when he passed on. I reviewed his finances with him and advised him on what to do in arranging his financial and personal affairs for an easier transition upon his death. He is now gone, but she has fond memories of him and now, thanks to her thoughtful husband, has enough financial resources to live comfortably for the rest of her life. Her husband made a top priority out of providing for her future.

Last night, Lynn and I decided to go to bed early and read. Warm blankets and reading seemed like a great way to relax and end a busy day. I have a stack of newsletters, magazines, books and commentaries, and my Bible on my nightstand. I was right in the middle of a good book on manly men and was about five minutes into reading it. Lynn finished reading a newsletter from a well-known and respected Christian evangelistic organization. She put down the newsletter and said she wanted to talk about something important. I put down my book and told her to go ahead. She then asked me whether there would be enough money for her to send to Christian organizations over and above any tithing to our church if I were to die before her. I thought for a second and said it depends on when I die. The sooner I die, the more insurance money there is for her. I then explained the plan I had been executing for the last several years in which all of our financial decisions centered around setting aside enough money for her to live on if I were to precede her in death. It is a real probability that she will outlive me. Her family is long-lived. Many of them lived into their nineties. Lynn has high amounts of good cholesterol (HDL), which some believe is a predictor of long life. This is an awesome opportunity for me with profound consequences. I am responsible for prudently setting aside enough money for her to live on should I die before her.

Losing a spouse is difficult and requires a tremendous amount of adjustment. Never having lost a spouse, I do not know how it feels. I have friend who unexpectedly lost his wife after a botched medical procedure. He told me I would never know what kind of an adjustment he had been going through during the three years since this happened. He said to me, “No one knows how I feel in this loss unless he has had a similar one.” He was right. I can have compassion for him, but I have not experienced his loss.

Another friend lost his wife to cancer on her fortieth birthday. She died at home. He was holding her in his arms when she adoringly looked at him and whispered, “I love you.” With that, she slipped into the everlasting arms of Jesus. He had the assurances of 2 Corinthians 5:6–8:

> Therefore we are always confident, knowing that, whilst we are at home in the body, we are

> absent from the Lord: (For we walk by faith, not by sight:) We are confident, I say, and willing rather to be absent from the body, and to be present with the Lord.

These men can relate to each other's losses, but I can only speculate on how they feel and what they have gone through.

Many years ago, at age thirty-eight, I quit my job and took the summer off to recover from a stress-related heart attack. I had a work area in my family room that overlooked the valley below our house. Our house was approximately three hundred feet above the valley. We lived in the hills, and there was a busy highway at the bottom of our property. We had trails carved out that allowed us to reach the bottom. I kept our horses down there in a corral. During the day, I devoted several hours to writing. With a book deadline, I scheduled myself to complete a certain number of pages each day in order to submit the manuscript to the publisher on time.

One morning, I was sitting at my desk writing when I heard a thundering crash and screaming. I went outside and saw that a large trash truck had come off the hill, gone across the highway, scraped the roof off a car, and landed on its side. The truck obviously had been speeding and had not negotiated a sharp curve higher up the hill. I immediately ran down the trail and saw a middle-aged man and a young woman running up to the flattened car. The woman who had been driving that car was his wife and her mother. I instinctively intercepted them and grabbed the daughter and held her back from the crushed car, and another man grabbed the father and likewise restrained him. None of us spoke a word, but we knew it was important that they not see their obviously deceased wife and mother in the car. I had no words of comfort and could only hold onto that young lady and give her comfort by simply being there.

We later found out the family had been caravanning in three separate cars, driving up the hill to their business, when this trash truck crashed through the barrier and ended the life of their wife and mother. Two things were important for me as a bystander. First, I needed to protect the family from seeing something horrific, and secondly, I had to simply be there. I believe it would have been a mistake for me to attempt words of comfort. The carnage and shock of this was too great for words. We need to ask the Lord for wisdom on how to respond to people in a crisis.

People have a tendency to look for a reason for their loss of a loved one when it is out of their control. Oftentimes we don't know why a loved one was taken away from us unexpectedly. Today, I had a young widow come into my office. She told me that two years ago, her husband was driving to work, the road iced, and he fatally crashed his car. He was in his peak of career productivity. Immediately all of their plans were changed. She told me it had taken her two years to get adjusted, and she still has her moments of despair. She did not seem bitter but was at a loss for why something like this could happen to her husband, who was so productive and enjoyed life.

Naomi became bitter because of her losses. She thought God was mad at her for something she did. "...the hand of the Lord is gone out against me." (Ruth 1:13). We can feel anger and bitterness out of perceived injustice. Like Naomi, we could blame ourselves and think God is punishing us. In Psalm 37:7, David gave us good advice: "Rest in the Lord, and wait patiently for him." Through David, the Lord was telling us not to worry and to depend on Him.

God may not reveal the purpose for a person's grief. There are times when He does so, but it may take years for one to know the purpose, and sometimes, one never knows it. We have to trust that God is in control. Our finite thinking cannot fully comprehend the greatness and character of God. We do get a glimpse of His character in Psalm 19. This psalm tells us the following:

- His glory and majesty are in His creation.
- The law of the Lord is perfect.
- The testimony of the Lord is sure.
- The statutes of the Lord are right.
- The commandment of the Lord is pure.
- The fear of the Lord is clean.
- The judgments of the Lord are true.
- The Lord is our strength and our Redeemer.

During times of extreme difficulty, distress, and grief, we need Scripture to help us. Sometimes people feel like they have been exiled by God. Isaiah 41:10 provides comfort in the assurance that the Lord is at hand.

Fear thou not, for I am with thee;

Be not dismayed, for I am thy God:

I will strengthen thee;

Yea, I will help thee;

Yea, I will uphold thee with the right hand of my righteousness.

CHAPTER 3

Journey Home

Wherefore she went out from the place where she was, and her two daughters in law with her; and they went on the way to return to the land of Judah. And Naomi said to her two daughters in law, Go, return each to her mother's house: the Lord deal kindly with you, as ye have dealt with the dead, and with me. The Lord grant that ye may find rest, each of you in the house of her husband. Then she kissed them; and they lifted up their voice, and wept. And they said to her, Surely we will return with thee unto thy people. And Naomi said, Turn again, my daughters: why will ye go with me? Are there yet any more sons in my womb, that they may be your husbands? Turn again, my daughters, go your way; for I am too old to have an husband. If I should say I have hope, if I should have an husband also tonight, and should also bear sons; Would ye tarry for them till they were grown? Would ye stay for them from having husbands? Nay, my daughters; for it grieveth me much for your

> sakes that the hand of the Lord is gone out against me. And they lifted up their voice, and wept again: and Orpah kissed her mother in law; but Ruth clave unto her. And she said, Behold thy sister in law is gone back unto her people and unto her gods: return thou after thy sister in law."
>
> —Ruth 1:7–15

Naomi's grief due to her losses clouded her reasoning. Her two daughters-in-law were willing to go to Bethlehem with her and face the unknown. They wanted to be with her despite facing an uncertain outcome. This indicates they had a wonderful relationship with Naomi. They were loyal to her and wanted to share in her future in Bethlehem. When Naomi insisted they stay in Moab and find husbands, she truthfully told them she was too old to provide sons for them. What Naomi could not see was that they wanted to be with her. When Orpah finally decided to stay in Moab, Ruth clung to Naomi. Still, Naomi told Ruth to go to her people and her gods as Orpah had done. This was a spiritual failing for Naomi. She encouraged Ruth to go and worship pagan gods instead of the true God of Israel. But Ruth knew this was not right. You wonder how Ruth found out about the true and living God. Was it things Naomi said or the example set in Naomi's household by both her and her late husband? We do not know, but Ruth knew that the God Naomi worshipped was the true God.

> And Ruth said, Intreat me not to leave thee, or to return from following after thee: For whither thou goest, I will go; and where thou lodgest, I will lodge: thy people shall be my people and thy God, my God. Where thou diest, will I die, and there will I be buried. The Lord do so to me, and more also, if ought but death parts you and me. When she saw that she was stedfastly minded to go with her, then she left speaking unto her. (Ruth 1:16–18)

At this point Naomi ceases to talk with Ruth even though Ruth makes seven decisions and commitments here. In the Scriptures, the number seven means completeness. Her complete decisions are as follows:

1. Where Naomi went, Ruth would go.

2. Where Naomi lodged, Ruth would lodge.

3. Naomi's people would be Ruth's people.
4. Naomi's God would be Ruth's God.
5. Where Naomi died, Ruth would die.
6. Where Naomi was buried, Ruth would be buried.
7. Only death would part Naomi and Ruth.

This is quite a list of promises Ruth made to Naomi. She kept them. If engaged couples made this list of promises to each other as wedding vows and kept them, we would have a lower divorce rate in our society.

Ruth was definitely stepping out in faith. She was inclined to travel anywhere with Naomi and experience everything she was about to experience, both the bad and the good. Ruth was ready to sleep on the side of the road as they travelled. She was of a mind to live in whatever house was available to them when they arrived in Bethlehem. She did not demand a large house in a prestigious community. She only wanted to be with Naomi and help her. Ruth was prepared to risk rejection by the Israelites, who historically despised Ruth's people. This was an unconditional love from Ruth toward Naomi's people, and yet she had not met them. Ruth knew there was something truthful about Naomi's God, and she wanted to worship Him.

Many Christians do not realize the influence they have on others through their actions. Non-Christians learn about our God through our actions. Our core beliefs are exhibited through our actions and leave an impact on others.

Fathers and mothers who are willing to carry through and make sure their kids get into church and Sunday school, learn from their Bible, and get tucked in with a prayer every night will have a better chance of making a positive, lasting impression of their beliefs on their children. Parents must also practice unconditional love and acceptance and not be legalistic toward their children.

I wonder if Elimelech was one of those fathers who was the spiritual leader of his home and prayed with his family. Ruth wanted to stay with Naomi until her death and share her burial site. This indicates that Naomi must have been a warm and kind person and exhibited actions that showed Ruth that her God was worth following.

A couple of times a year, I visit the national veterans' cemetery at Fort Rosecrans in San Diego, California. I have an uncle buried there and honor his memory and those of thousands of veterans during my visit. My uncle was a World War II pilot who flew the "Hump" over Burma and was highly decorated. In addition to many other medals for bravery, he received the Distinguished Flying Cross twice. Sometimes I look around and find the grave of a veteran with inscriptions of his name, date of death, and wife's name—without her own date of death. In these situations, the couple has made a covenant to share the same grave as a statement of their undying love for each other, and the wife has not made it there yet.

Ruth's commitment to go with Naomi and stay with her until death was one of her purposes as orchestrated by God. The Lord called her to go with Naomi to Bethlehem. Many years later, in Nazareth, the angel Gabriel, which means "man of God," came to Mary and told her about her calling to serve the Lord. Her response to Gabriel was "Behold, the handmaid of the Lord; be it unto me according to thy word" (Luke 1:38). Jesus, a descendant of Ruth, was born in Bethlehem.

Once Naomi accepted that Ruth was going, they secured their belongings and began the long walk to Bethlehem. Whatever they owned, they carried with them. They journeyed in the springtime. We know this because of the barley harvest in Bethlehem. A difficult fifty-mile journey awaited them. The trails or roads took them through rough terrain. Cold nights and hot days were ahead of them. There obviously were no conveniences along the way. They would have to ration any food and water they had taken with them. They were vulnerable to robbery, wild animals, and other treachery along the way.

Naomi exuded bitterness during the trip. With each step she took in the direction of Bethlehem, thoughts bombarded her about what God had done to her by taking away her husband and two sons. Our thought lives are important. In Naomi's situation, she remained captive to thoughts of bitterness, as she believed God was punishing her. There is no indication that she sought out the Lord through prayer, fasting, and supplication. She continued her journey as a bitter widow. Naomi's bitterness overshadowed her recognition of the sovereignty of God. The Lord had blessings for her in His time. She lacked trust in His ability to care for her.

In Psalm 68:4–8, Ruth's descendant, King David, praised the Lord and affirmed His provisions:

> Sing unto God, sing praises to his name; Extol him that rideth upon the heavens, by his name JAH, and rejoice before him. A father of the fatherless, and a judge of the widows, Is God in his holy habitation. God setteth the solitary in families: He bringeth out those which are bound with chains: but the rebellious dwell in a dry land. O God, when thou wentest forth before thy people, When thou didst march through the wilderness; Selah: The earth shook; the heavens also dropped at the presence of God: Even Sinai itself was moved at the presence of God, the God of Israel.

One could imagine Ruth comforting Naomi along the way. Picture Naomi, about ten miles out, stopping to rest on a rock. She is miserable; her feet are hurting, she has pebbles in her sandals, she is thirsty, her body aches, and her countenance is disconsolate. A loyal and caring Ruth puts down her bundle and walks over to help Naomi. She takes some scarce water and wipes Naomi's face. She then removes Naomi's sandals, shakes out the pebbles, and then washes her feet. As she gives Naomi a drink, she strokes Naomi's hair in adoration and gives her words of encouragement. Ruth blessed Naomi as a companion.

> So they two went until they came to Bethlehem. And it came to pass, when they were come to Bethlehem, that all the city was moved about them, and they said, "Is this Naomi?" and she said unto them, "call me not Naomi, call me Mara; and the Almighty hath dealt very bitterly with me. I went out full and the Lord has brought me home again empty: Why then call me Naomi, seeing the Lord has testified against me, and the Almighty has afflicted me?" So Naomi returned, and Ruth the Moabitess her daughter in law with her, which returned out of the country of Moab: and they came to Bethlehem at the beginning of the barley harvest. (Ruth 1:19–22)

Naomi received a warm reception from the women of Bethlehem when she arrived. They came out, greeted her, and showed their thankfulness that she had returned. There were probably tears and hugs of joy from those who were glad to see her after her ten-year absence. The community immediately accepted her. However, her response indicated grief as she lamented her loss. She adopted the name Mara, which means "bitter." She wanted everyone to know that she thought God was punishing her through the loss of her husband and two sons. She never said what she thought she had done to deserve punishment. Sometimes the Lord allows events in our lives for correction and other times for direction. In Naomi's case, it could have been for direction.

This is a stark contrast to how Job responded to his devastating circumstances. When disaster struck him, he said:

> Naked came I out of my mother's womb, And naked shall I return thither: The Lord gave, and the Lord hath taken away; Blessed be the name of the Lord. (Job 1:21)

Job had just lost his oxen, donkeys, sheep, camels, servants, seven sons, and three daughters. Yet he was still able to say, "Blessed be the name of the Lord."

Job later lost his health, and he did ask God why all of this was happening to him. It is not wrong to ask why; however, it is wrong to question and make accusations against the sovereignty of God. Job stayed true to God.

In all this Job sinned not, nor charged God foolishly. (Job 1:22)

Job obviously had a close walk with God before this happened. In all of his adversity, he trusted God's sovereignty.

What? Shall we receive good at the hand of God, and shall we not receive evil? In all this did not Job sin with his lips. (Job 2:10)

When we face adversity, we need to acknowledge God and look for his purpose in our lives. A believer will trust in God through prosperity or adversity, even while unable to understand why bad things happen. God may allow adversity to happen in our lives as a chastening and correction, or He may be providentially orchestrating events to our long-term benefit. We all face adversity at times and need to accept it as part of life's experiences. God cares for us and he always has our best interest in mind.

Naomi told the women that she came home empty. Here we have Ruth standing by her, probably a little further back to her side, and Naomi is not acknowledging her presence. Evidently the loss of her husband and two sons' was causing her to feel empty. Naomi still has not recognized that Ruth is a gift from the Lord, but will soon find out that her travel companion is just what the Lord wanted her to bring home. Naomi is still oblivious at this point on what the Lord is orchestrating for her and Ruth.

I have had my share of disappointments. I worked the night shift full-time at Hughes Aircraft Company for seven years while I put myself through school. Additionally, on the weekends, I had a part-time job as an emergency cryptographer handling top secret communication for the air force at the same location in Culver City, California. During that time, I averaged around three to five hours sleep a night. I supported a wife and two children. I went from a being non-college-prepared student to having master's degree in those seven years. I was always on time for work and had an excellent work record. I never missed a day of work.

During my last year of university studies, I applied for a special job with Hughes. They usually hired six MBA graduates each year and put them through a two-year development program. I signed up for an interview on campus and met with the recruiter. He immediately put me on the A list for their one-day on-site interview. I arrived at the interview location early on the appointed morning and waited until five minutes before the appointment to go to the proper floor. It was a Hughes site approximately five miles from my job location. I wore a business suit and used my badge to get into the facility. My top-secret crypto clearance gave me access to all facilities.

As I sat in the waiting room, I saw this midforties woman nervously running around and impatiently pressing the elevator button so she could hurry up to the next floor. It was obvious she belonged to the interview team. She desperately attempted to take care of last-minute details. I did not bother her and sat patiently until I was called. She finally came up to me and wanted to know who I was. I told her I was a candidate. She looked at my badge and said, "Just because you already work here doesn't mean we will hire you." This was not a good way for me to start an interview day for what I considered a dream job for an MBA. As it turned out that day, I had another manager give me a bad time. He was young, arrogant, and rude. I remained polite to both of them. The other managers I interviewed with that day were polite and professional. At lunch they assigned us to interviewers tasked to screen the candidates further. I found it difficult to get traction in the discussion. Never mind that I had gotten home at 1:00 a.m. that morning and gotten back up at 5:00 a.m. I had difficulty breaking into the conversation. The interviewer focused on the other two candidates.

A couple of weeks later, I took a forty-five-minute nap in the afternoon prior to getting ready for work. Lynn woke me up. She was holding an opened letter and gave me a hug and said, “I’m sorry.” It was a rejection letter from Hughes. I had faithfully worked for this company seven long years, had an excellent record, just finished my MBA at a prestigious school, and was not good enough for their development program. I later found out that in trying to be polite and not overbearing, I was deemed not forceful enough. It felt like an arrow struck through my heart. I found it difficult to accept this rejection at first. But I knew the Lord had a reason for closing that door, and I needed to take it by faith. I thanked Hughes for seven years of employment and left knowing I had experienced a stepping-stone to something better, and the Lord did not want me to stay there.

I soon found out that as the Lord closes one door, and he opens another. He was reserving a divine appointment for me. A wonderful executive at another major corporation interviewed and hired me as a business analyst with no specific job assignment. He gave me an opportunity to learn business that I would have never experienced at Hughes. My new job was unstructured. I brought ideas for study to my boss for cost savings and better business practices. My results had a positive impact on the company. This turned out to be the best experience any recent MBA graduate could possibly receive.

CHAPTER 4
Vertical Purposes

> And Naomi had a kinsman of her husband's, a mighty man of wealth, of the family of Elimelech; and his name was Boaz. And Ruth the Moabitess said unto Naomi, Let me now go to the field, and glean ears of corn after him in whose sight I shall find grace. And she said to her, Go, my daughter. (Ruth 2:1–2)

Ruth wanted to secure food for herself and Naomi. She recognized the importance of getting above her circumstances and conquering any obstacles. This was in the spring, when the barley harvest was in full production. Workers were out in the fields busily harvesting the grain.

God commanded the people to care for widows and orphans. The owners of fields had to allow widows and poor people to glean in the fields after the harvesters were finished gathering. This command is given in Leviticus 19:9-10 and Deuteronomy 24:19. The harvesters were not able to gather every grain, and therefore, some would fall on the ground and be available for gleaners.

Ruth wisely sought Naomi's permission to glean in the fields. Evidently, Ruth knew about the law of Moses that made gleaning available to widows. She wanted to get food for both of them.

> And she went, and came, and gleaned in the field after the reapers. And her hap was to light on a part of the field belonging unto Boaz, who was of the kindred of Elimelech. (Ruth 2:3)

Ruth was not targeting a particular field, but through God's providential guidance, she ended up in Boaz's field, and he noticed her. Boaz was a man of great wealth, an eligible bachelor, and a relative of Naomi's late husband, Elimelech. Boaz was the son of Salmon and Rahab, the harlot who lived in Jericho and helped Joshua when he was spying on the city. Joshua was getting ready to attack Jericho and needed her help. She became a believer in the true and living God of Israel. Because of her help to Joshua and her faith in God, she and her family were saved from destruction when Joshua attacked and destroyed Jericho. She was a brave woman who did what was right at great risk to her life. She was taken out of an unholy circumstance and placed into a holy place.

> And behold, Boaz came from Bethlehem, and said unto the reapers, The Lord be with you. And they answered him, The Lord bless thee. (Ruth 2:4)

Boaz was a high-caliber manager and leader. He made sure he visited the reapers and gave them a blessing for the day. The response to his greeting says a lot about his character. The reapers answered by saying, "The Lord bless thee." His employees respected and held him in high esteem. Boaz showed a genuine concern and encouraged them during their long workday. The barley harvest season lasted about six weeks. The workers began at dawn each day and ended their work at dusk.

> Then said Boaz unto his servant that was set over the reapers, Whose damsel is this? (Ruth 2:5)

Boaz was still making the rounds, greeting his employees and checking on all the logistics for the day, such as drinking water and other provisions for the workers, when he saw Ruth. Her overall countenance probably made his heart rush. Her presence captivated him. This could have been love at first sight. After all, the Lord had orchestrated this otherwise chance meeting. Boaz was single and had waited on the Lord to provide him a wife. Some men fall for women based solely on their looks and can get disappointed. Others are wiser, seek to know the character of a woman, and make a decision as to whether or not to pursue her based on more than just looks. I know average-looking women who captivate men with their positive and friendly personalities. Our culture places too much emphasis on physical attractiveness. In any case, Boaz liked her countenance. Now he wanted to know more about her.

> And the servant who was set over the reapers answered and said, It is the Moabitish damsel that came back with Naomi out of the country of Moab. And she said, I pray you, let me glean and gather after the reapers among the sheaves: so she came, and hath continued even from the morning until now, that she tarried a little in the house. (Ruth 2:6–7)

Ruth was gathering food in Boaz's fields, and the workers reported that she had been working hard all morning. Boaz watched as she continued to gather up gleanings from the field. At this point, one could imagine him asking the Lord, "Is this the one for me?" He was evidently older than she and had been waiting a long time for the Lord to provide him with a wife. With his maturity, position, and wealth in the community, he could have married a long time before this.

God uses interactions with other people in our lives to help us attain what He wants for us. In this situation, he brought Ruth to Boaz. God was orchestrating His purposes for Ruth and Boaz. Both of them were willing to listen to Him and take further instructions. God does not use people in our lives to help us attain what we want to do, only what He wants for His purposes. As we see with Ruth and Boaz, He brought them together to do what He wanted them to do and thereby accomplish His purposes.

Boaz and Ruth were willing by faith to give their all and follow the Lord's leading in their lives. When God has something for you to do, He will know where to find you. Be prepared because He can call you at any time with an assignment as He did with Ruth and Boaz. You must be willing to give your all to the Lord. Our society today tells people to self-realize and pursue their own interests. But the Lord requires us to commit ourselves to Him in full self-expenditure to serve Him.

I am always interested in finding out where married couples met. I met my wife in a bookkeeping class. Even though I was sixteen, it was love at first sight. Some couples meet in restaurants, on planes, in the workplace, at church, during social events, through mutual friends, or in a wide range of other ways. Most of us know married couples who met online. All of these first-time meetings have something in common. Each person looks at the other and makes an immediate assessment as to social compatibility. This is not necessarily marriage compatibility. Each of us projects an aura of our personality when others see us. During my first meeting with my wife, I sensed she had deep, caring qualities and was genuine. She sensed that I was responsible and consistent and had a purpose. We dated for two years before getting married. During this time, we were able to test each other and make sure these qualities had staying power.

A relationship that starts out with quality interaction and minimal physical contact has a better chance of reaching deep roots of respect and understanding. I see some young people hanging all over each other. This usually occurs at the beginning stages of a relationship. Unless they develop good communication and mutual respect, a low probability of success will follow.

Today, we have fewer young men than in previous decades willing to take on the responsibility of marrying a girl and caring for her. They would rather move in with a girl, receive the benefits of marriage, and leave her when circumstances are no longer favorable. Unfortunately, many fathers are not protecting their daughters from these kinds of young men.

Boaz was ready for marriage. He waited until he was mature and established in his business. He was most likely older than most men are when they marry. But younger men can have the same credentials as Boaz. Ruth was at a prime age for marrying. What are the qualities Boaz possessed?

As the story unfolds, we will find out more about him. He was a godly man who turned each day over to the Lord. Boaz's qualities are what a woman should look for when contemplating marriage. As we learn more about Boaz, we will see the following in him:

- a heart for God
- qualities of the heart (empathy and compassion)
- maturity
- spiritual Leadership qualities
- workplace leadership (as a business owner, he inspired others)
- servant leadership
- a caring spirit
- good financial management
- industrious work ethic
- honesty
- forward thinking (he anticipated things and took action ahead of time)
- critical thinking
- common sense
- generosity
- friendliness
- alertness
- responsibility
- commitment

- fairness in dealing with others
- a kind heart

This is a long list of qualities to work on. If we seek out the Lord and ask for His help, He will guide us and help us develop these qualities over time. Studying the Bible and praying often are good starters.

What are the qualities Boaz saw in Ruth? He observed her working diligently in the field, and later in the day, he interacted with her during lunch. He found her to be the following:

- industrious and hard working
- humble
- friendly
- caring
- faithful
- honoring
- generous
- productive
- committed
- kindhearted
- spiritually tuned into God
- alert

Ruth was careful to make use of her time by gathering food for her and Naomi.

Like Ruth, men and women need to redeem their time and concentrate on good things. Ask yourself, “What am I doing with my time? Do I use it for meaningful purposes? Am I wasting my time pursuing something that is meaningless?” Life is a pilgrimage, and we have control over our spare time and what we do with it. Find yourself companions who are like-minded toward improving themselves and set out in a positive direction. If you are serious about becoming a better person, avoid time-wasting pursuits and concentrate on self-improvement. This includes immersing yourself in the Word to know God better.

I was not prepared for marriage at the age of eighteen and had to learn things fast. Some of the Boaz qualities took me years to develop. It is still a work in progress. I learned quickly that marriage requires the consideration of the feelings, thoughts, aspirations, values, and desires of two people. I had to learn to consider my wife in all things. I can remember a fellow in our young marrieds’ Sunday school class telling me that he had gotten in trouble with his wife. He decided on his own to order all-new furniture for their home without consulting his wife. He had not even thought to ask her about this large purchase. When the furniture arrived, his wife got madder as each piece was unloaded. He ended up sleeping on the new couch that night. I suggested he sit down with her, ask her forgiveness, and let her decide what to do with the furniture. This is a good example of the importance of taking your spouse's feelings into consideration. It may seem simple, but we all have our shortcomings. I have a long list of things I have done that impacted my wife and I did not think of her until after my actions. Now I try to involve her in everything, including business decisions.

Dating is important in helping you to see a potential spouse in various settings and his or her reactions to events. Sometimes it takes two years or more for this to play out enough to get a good idea of a person's overall character. Older couples may find a shorter time frame is workable.

Every first quarter of the year, because of my practice, I sit down with several hundred couples and spend a half hour to an hour with each one. Some of the couples seem to blend well and have seamless communication. At the opposite end are those who stumble while communicating and have trouble understanding each other. It is evident that those who communicate well spend a lot of time talking face-to-face. They know how to listen, probe, discuss, and disagree. I find it important to talk face-to-face with my wife. Over the years, I developed a bad habit of saying something and then walking to another room with her response trailing me. This incomplete transaction often led to a misunderstanding. This is because I talked and did not stick around to listen. I now make sure we acknowledge each other's comments. During the time couples get to know each other, they should be developing good communication practices. I see successful marriages when this happens.

When Boaz met Ruth, there was a purpose to their meeting, as God had a plan for them. Eternal values were at play because God as a Redeemer chose Boaz to be a redeemer. God chose Ruth to be in the line of Christ. When couples meet, it is a good idea for them to ask themselves what the purpose for their meeting is. When couples meet only for pleasure, trouble will follow.

I had a father tell me his daughter's boyfriend was planning on taking her to another state, where they were going to live together. The father asked the boy about his intentions for his daughter. The boy could not give him a cogent answer. The father let her go anyway. The boy's intentions were obvious. He was up to no good. The daughter eventually came home after the boyfriend got what he wanted out of her. This father was not protective. He did not hold this boy accountable. He should have signaled his disapproval and told the boy to stay away.

Boaz's intentions were honorable. He was a man of purpose who followed the Lord. He also was willing to be held accountable to the elders in his community. Boaz had a God-given conscience. He knew how to be an honorable man and maintain the dignity of a woman.

Women should not have to protect themselves. But there are times when they must. My dad's mother was a sweet-spirited and kind woman. She had fifteen children and was a wonderful mother and grandmother. My grandparents' home was a block away from a railroad stop. Many times, hobos knocked at their front door asking for a hot meal. My grandmother eagerly reached out to them and gave them food. The only time I ever heard her yell was when she got mad at my grandfather for being drunk during our visit to their home. My sweet grandmother also carried a loaded derringer in her apron. I recently got the answer to why she carried this weapon. I visited their youngest daughter's husband a few years ago, and he told me he had asked my grandmother about the pistol. "To keep my honor" was her reply. I put the pieces together in talking with other family members. When she was a young woman, her boss at the woolen mill violated her. What a difference between her boss and Boaz. Boaz would never have taken advantage of a woman. Women do not have to protect themselves from honorable men. Fortunately, there are godly young men out there like Boaz. If a woman is dating a man who isn't like Boaz, she should keep looking.

CHAPTER 5

A Man and His Role

> Then said Boaz unto Ruth, Hearest thou not, my daughter? Go not to glean in another field, neither go from hence, but abide here fast by my maidens: Let thine eyes be on the field that they do reap, and go thou after them: have I not charged the young men that they shall not touch thee? And when thou are athirst, go unto the vessels and drink that which what the young men have drawn." (Ruth 2:8–9)

Men have a special role in life. They are to be the protectors and providers for their families. This is the basic definition of love. It provides a tremendous responsibility and opportunity. They are also to be the spiritual leaders in their households. It is not surprising that Boaz knew his role. He was a man of God. He knew God as a Redeemer and provider. He knew God purposed men to do the same for their wives.

Verses eight and nine show his understanding of how to provide for and protect a woman. He wanted to make sure Ruth knew she was welcome in his fields and was under his protection. He instructed his young men to stay away from her and allow her to drink from their water supply. Obviously, a man cannot provide for every woman in need, but they can be sensitive to needs in the community.

There are men who take great pleasure in providing for their wives, while others resent it or outright reject it. I know this is an oversimplification, but I see two basic relationships in a marriage. The traditional one is the "A" relationship. Think of each vertical of the "A" leaning on the other with the horizontal bar representing a relationship. In this relationship, the husband and wife depend on each other in defined, traditional roles. The husband is the provider and protector, and the wife is the keeper of the household.

The husband is the chief executive officer, and the wife is the chief operating officer. The husband is not abusive, authoritarian, or arbitrary. He is to love his wife.

> Husbands, love your wives, even as Christ also loved the church, and gave himself for it. (Ephesians 5:25)

The husband is responsible for any decisions he makes when the two of them cannot agree on an issue. In this traditional view, the husband is to love and honor his wife. He is no better than her and must seek her counsel on all matters.

An extreme "H" relationship has each spouse on an economic stand-alone basis. The vertical lines represent their independence from each other. The horizontal line across the "H" represents their relationship. There is a defined communication and emotional tie between husband and wife in this marriage. Love and mutual attraction brought them together. Each one has a career and his or her own checking account. They usually divide the household financial obligations according to an agreed formula. Each of them is free to take separate vacations and have friends to the exclusion of the other spouse. For some couples who marry late in life and have demanding careers, this is an optional marital arrangement. It allows them to have a limited marriage relationship with a great deal of personal and financial freedom.

Some older couples marry after each losing a spouse. They may decide to keep their assets separate due to estate and inheritance issues. This is not the kind of "H" relationship I am talking about.

For young couples getting married, the "H" relationship is not good when the husband tells the wife she must leave the children in day care, support herself, and pay half of the bills.

Today, each of these may appear extreme. Many married couples fall somewhere in between the two. Boaz providing for Ruth and Naomi was a good example. Grown men are diverse in their levels of maturity. Some men are not ready for marriage. They cannot even take care of themselves, let alone a wife. Others gladly take on a wife and want to support her financially, spiritually, and physically.

I know a man who was a US Army combat sergeant and served in Austria toward the end of World War II. He told me the wonderful love story of how he met his wife. This young sergeant was in a village and noticed a group of women prisoners of war who had just been liberated. They were Ukrainian and had been in forced labor camps and were being led into a secure garrison until the US military could repatriate them.

As the women walked down the road in front of this sergeant, he noticed one who had a radiant countenance and seemed upbeat despite the awful circumstances she had endured. He pointed her out to one of his soldiers and said, "I want to marry her." The other soldier probably thought his sergeant was just homesick. But this was not the case.

After the women were locked in the compound, he went up to the sentry and demanded to be let in. The sentry denied his request, so the sergeant pulled out his .45-caliber pistol, shot off the lock, and entered. The sentry was speechless. He could have shot the sergeant. However, the sentry relented. The sergeant outranked him by several stripes.

The sergeant found the woman he wanted in the crowd, talked with her, and began a lifelong love story with her. They have been married since 1945, and he still treats her like she is a queen. She has benefitted from a wonderful life and has reciprocated this to her husband. The marriage benefitted from his strong leadership, which included unconditional love and caring for his life partner. This former sergeant took responsibility for her welfare beginning on day one of their marriage. Today, they are both in declining health, and she is suffering from dementia. She does not recognize many people or remember many things. But when she sees him, her face lights up, and she beams a radiant smile.

Boaz made a lifelong commitment to Ruth. It was not a commitment of convenience, but a lasting relationship built on principles. God, as a leader, guided Boaz in natural ways, and Boaz willingly followed Him. God called on Boaz to practice management, leadership, ethics, kindness, obedience, and commitment in all his transactions, including marriage. This was a profound responsibility. Boaz paid attention, managed the affairs of his family, and looked out for their needs. He was a leader in his home. He took up the spiritual mantle and made sure they were grounded in the things of the Lord. Boaz obeyed the Lord and His commands and instructions.

> Then she fell on her face, and bowed herself to the ground, and said unto him, Why have I found grace in thine eyes, that thou shouldest take knowledge of me, seeing I am a stranger? And Boaz answered and said unto her, It hath fully been shewed me, all that thou hath done

> unto thy mother in law since the death of thine husband: and how thou has left thy father and thy mother and the land of thy nativity, and art come unto a people which thou knewest not heretofore. The Lord recompense thy work, and a full reward be given thee of the Lord God of Israel, under whose wings thou are come to trust. (Ruth 2:10–12)

Boaz took Ruth under his wing and became her protector and provider for a lifetime. He may have inquired at the gates of the city regarding Ruth. He got the whole story right on her background and circumstances. He liked what he heard about her. He could discern that she was a quality person. He affirmed the Lord's protection over her and added that the Lord would give her a full reward for her kindness to Naomi. He acknowledged that the Lord God of Israel was providing refuge and protection for Ruth. He understood the character of God and closely followed Him.

Boaz was under the protection and blessing of God. He was God's servant and understood his role in carrying out the will of God in all that he did. He was also a gifted leader and manager. His good stewardship of what God provided to him was evident in his actions.

> Then she said, Let me find favor in thy sight, my lord; for that thou hast comforted me, and for that thou hast spoken friendly unto thy handmaid, though I be not like one of thine handmaids. And Boaz said unto her, at mealtime, Come thou hither, and eat of the bread, and dip thy morsel in the vinegar. And she sat beside the reapers: and he reached her parched corn, and she did eat, and was sufficed, and left. (Ruth 2:13–14)

At mealtime, Boaz made sure Ruth ate with him. Notice that he had her sit beside his reapers. He was showing good leadership by eating with his employees. He let them know he cared for them and that they were valued as his employees.

> And when she was risen up to glean, Boaz commanded his young men, saying, Let her glean even among the sheaves, and reproach her not: And let fall also some of the handfuls of purpose for her, and leave them, that she may glean them, and rebuke her not. (Ruth 2:15–16)

Handfuls of purpose is key to the book of Ruth. Through Boaz, the Lord gave both Ruth and Naomi handfuls of purpose. What He was giving them was far more than food. The Lord gives all who seek Him handfuls of purpose. Through His Son, Jesus, He gave us redemption and salvation. Boaz later became a kinsman-redeemer for Ruth and Naomi. Jesus is a kinsman-redeemer for all who will believe in Him. Boaz provided that which represented the bread of life as a gracious gift to his soon-to-be-bride. In this Boaz represents Christ and Ruth represents each believer destined for a union with Christ. The sheaves represent the Word of God from which we can daily glean life giving food for our souls. God provides us with handfuls of purpose in the fruitful field of His Word.

"I rejoice at thy word, as one that findeth great spoil." Psalm 119:162

> So she gleaned in the field until even, and beat out that she had gleaned: and it was about an ephah of barley. (Ruth 2:17)

An ephah of barley was enough to feed Ruth and Naomi for about five days. It was quite a bundle for her to carry home to Naomi.

> And she took it up, and went into the city: and her mother in law saw what she had gleaned: and she brought forth, and gave to her that she had reserved after she was sufficed. (Ruth 2:18)

Ruth also gave Naomi the food she had kept when she was eating with Boaz and the reapers. This was another indicator of Ruth's character. She was a generous person and cared about others.

> And her mother in law said unto her, Where hast thou gleaned today? And where wroughtest thou? Blessed be he that did take knowledge of thee. And she shewed her mother in law with whom she had wrought, and said, The man's name with whom I wrought today is Boaz (Ruth 2:19)

Naomi was interested in the day's events. You could imagine her eyes getting wider as Ruth told all that had happened that day. Ruth told her mother in law, with whom she had worked, and said, "The man's name with whom I worked today is Boaz." Naomi was awestruck. This was good news to her. Of all people, Boaz noticed Ruth. Naomi's bitterness was fading. She realized something profound was taking place in Ruth's life.

> And Naomi said to her daughter in law, Blessed be he of the Lord, who hath not left off his kindness to the living and to the dead! And Naomi said unto her, The man is near kin unto us., one of our next kinsmen. And Ruth the Moabitess said, He said unto me also, thou shall keep fast by my young men, until they have ended all my harvest. And Naomi said unto Ruth her daughter in law, It is good, my daughter, that thou go out with his maidens, that they meet thee not in any other field." (Ruth 2:20–22)

Finally, Naomi gave good advice. Earlier, things were dim to her, but she now saw the situation more clearly.

> So she kept fast by the maidens of Boaz, to glean until the end of the barley harvest and of wheat harvest; and dwelt with her mother in law. (Ruth 2:23).

Every evening when Ruth came home, no doubt Naomi was eagerly waiting outside for her. Naomi wanted to hear about each day's events. During this time, Naomi gathered up all her cups of bitterness and tossed them out. She probably looked out each morning as Ruth was leaving for the fields, sighed, and said, “The Lord is good.” Each night, she had the table set and the meal ready. Thanks to Ruth’s hard work and Boaz’s generosity, they had enough food to eat.

CHAPTER 6

A Man Proves His Worth

> Then Naomi her mother in law said unto her, My daughter, shall I not seek rest for thee, that it may be well with thee? And now is not Boaz of our kindred, whose maidens thou wast? Behold he winnoweth barley tonight in the threshing floor. Wash thyself therefore, and anoint thee, and put thy raiment upon thee, and get thee down to the floor: but make not thyself known unto the man, until he shall have done eating and drinking. And it shall be, when he lieth down, that thou shalt mark the place where he shall lie; and thou shalt go in, and uncover his feet, and lay thee down; and he will tell thee what thou shalt do. And she said to her, All that thou sayest unto me I will do. (Ruth 3:1–5)

The Lord was working on Naomi. She had a new role in life – advisor. Because of the advice she was dispensing to Ruth, she must have been close to the Lord, and was receiving her instructions from him. She was eager to bring Boaz and Ruth together. With her renewed purpose, she most likely woke up each morning and faced the events of the day with wonderful anticipation. The possible relationship of Boaz and Ruth brought new meaning to her life.

Naomi was a key part in this transaction. The Lord directed her steps and showed her what to do. Ruth highly respected Naomi and knew that she had knowledge about their culture that would be helpful to her. Naomi was familiar with the concept of kinsman-redeemer. Naomi prefaced her suggestions with the thought of looking out for Ruth's welfare and security for the future. She was building a case for Boaz to be their kinsman-redeemer.

Somehow, Naomi knew Boaz would be at the threshing floor that night. She had no doubt developed an informal grapevine of communication with other women in the community since coming back to Bethlehem. She had the place and timing down just right. Naomi knew Boaz needed to stay with his crops lest anyone steal them.

What Naomi said to Ruth was both instructive and prophetic. The Lord's wisdom was guiding her. In this conversation, Naomi told Ruth to do four things:

> Wash thyself therefore, and anoint thee, and put thy raiment upon thee, and get thee down to the floor. (Ruth 3:3)

These four things are indicative of a believer's relationship with Jesus. To wash ourselves is to ask forgiveness for our sins. To anoint ourselves is to open our spiritual eyes through the Holy Spirit. To wear our best garments is to cloak ourselves in the robe of Christ's righteousness. We put off our sinful past (Ephesians 4:22–24). Finally, the threshing floor represents our proper place of worship: at the Lord's feet.

Naomi instructed Ruth to make sure she knew where he would lay down for the night. No one was to see her until the right moment.

Ruth left Naomi and headed down the road and then up the hill to the threshing floor. So far no one had noticed her. She was careful to hide her face from the moonlight. Ruth quietly climbed the hill. Once there, she hid behind a shelter and surveyed the threshing floor and all the people walking back and forth. It did not take her long to spot Boaz.

All the while, her heart was probably racing faster than ever in anticipation of this evening's outcome. She continued to be inconspicuous. She surveyed the comings and goings and kept her eyes fixed on Boaz. She knew all was in the Lord's hands. Providentially He revealed the script to Naomi, who in turn passed it on to Ruth.

Naomi, waiting at home, was probably experiencing the most exhilaration she had sensed in many years. Naomi could now see why the previous events had to happen. She was now following the Lord as His servant.

> And she went down unto the floor, and did according to all that her mother in law bade her. And when Boaz had eaten and drunk, and his heart was merry, he went to lie down at the end of the heap of corn: and she came softly, and uncovered his feet, and laid her down. (Ruth 3:6–7)

Up to this point, no one knew that Ruth was present. The right time came, and she softly and quietly moved to the threshing floor. She positioned herself on the floor, uncovered his feet, and lay down. Suddenly Boaz felt a cold draft on his feet. Wiggling his feet around, he felt the warmth of somebody at his feet. It was providential that he did not shout and jump up and make a big commotion about this. Instead, he coolly looked down and saw a woman lying at his feet. Now he wanted to know who it was. He inquired, saw her face, and discovered, to his relief, that it was Ruth.

> And it came to pass at midnight, that the man was afraid, and turned himself: and, behold, a woman lay at his feet. And he said, Who art thou? And she answered, I am Ruth, thy handmaid: spread therefore thy skirt over thine handmaid; for thou art a near kinsman. (Ruth 3:8–9)

She then asked Boaz to take her under his wing and qualified it by saying he was a close relative. Previously, Boaz had praised Ruth for taking Naomi under her wing. Now it was Boaz's turn to take them under his wing. Everyone did his or her part in carrying out God's plan.

In the meantime, Naomi was probably sitting back at home, wondering how all of this was playing out. She most likely kept herself busy the whole night and could not sit still. She sat down and then got up and straightened out a vase and then sat down again. Then she got up again and brushed her graying hair. Then she sat down again. She checked the oil lamp and moved it to another table. She just could not sit still because of the high drama. All night she was both anxious and thrilled about these events and was eager to see how they were going to play out. She added more oil to the lamp and kept it burning and sat back waiting for any sound or stirring outside. She knew that the longer Ruth was gone, the better the circumstances.

It is unlikely that Boaz, Naomi, or Ruth slept much that night. The profound importance of this potential relationship was far-reaching.

> And he said, Blessed be thou of the Lord, my daughter: For thou hast shewed more kindness in the latter end than at the beginning, inasmuch as thou followest not young men, whether poor or rich. And now, my daughter, fear not; I will do to thee all that thou requirest: for all the city of my people doth know that thou art a virtuous woman. (Ruth 3:10–11)

No doubt, Boaz said, "Thank You, Lord." He blessed Ruth for showing kindness to him. She chose a man older than her. We don't know if he was previously married and lost his wife. But if he was not, he now knew why the Lord had had him wait all these years for a wife.

Boaz had to confront an issue that could get in the way of completing this transaction. But he was confident and steady. He was the kind of man Ruth needed. In fact, any woman who wants a man of substance would want a Boaz.

At this point, Boaz and Ruth probably felt like singing to each another an affirmation of their pent-up mutual feelings.

Many years ago, Bobby Worth wrote the song "Don't You Know?" Della Reese sang it. Imagine for a moment that she was singing on behalf of Boaz and Ruth, each to the other.

"Don't You Know?" talks about falling in love with someone and loving that person for one's whole lifetime. Ruth, through the Lord's leading, happened to come by the fields of Boaz. They were most likely captivated with each other when they met.

Lyrics

"Don't you know

I have fallen in love with you

For the rest of my whole life through

Don't you know

I was yours from the very day

That you happened to come my way

Can't you see

I'm under your spell

By the look in my eyes

Can't you tell, can't you tell

Now don't you know

Every beat of my heart keeps crying out

I want you so

Don't you know

Songwriter: Bobby Worth

Falling in love is a wonderful experience and a lifetime of love with the same person provides a completeness and fulfillment of God's purposes.

> And now it is true that I am thy near kinsman: howbeit there is a kinsman nearer than I. Tarry this night, and it shall be in the morning and it shall be that if he will perform the part of the kinsman, well; let him do the kinsman's part: but if he will not do the part of a kinsman to thee, then will I do the part of the kinsman to thee, as the Lord liveth: lie down until the morning. (Ruth 3:12–13)

Boaz promised that first thing in the morning he would find the close relative and get this issue resolved. He wanted Ruth for his wife and knew she was a gift from the Lord. Ruth had the same thoughts about Boaz. They were each thinking privately how wonderful it was for them to meet. The Lord created them for each other.

> And she lay at his feet until morning: and she arose before one could know another. And he said, Let it not be known that a woman came into the floor. Also he said, Bring the vail thou hast upon thee, and hold it. And when she held

> it, he measured six measures of barley, and laid it on her: and she went into the city. (Ruth 3:14–15)

Boaz provided protection for Ruth in several ways here. He told her to stay with him until morning. It was late at night, and she was safe with him. Additionally, he said to keep quiet about being there. He did not want any of the town gossips to hear about it and thereby diminish her character.

He gave her a large amount of barley to take home—a thirty-day supply. Boaz was generous and knew how to provide.

Early the next morning, before anyone else awoke, Ruth got up, made sure Boaz was covered by his blanket, picked up her barley sack, and headed home. She arrived home just as the sun came up. Naomi heard her outside and looked at the oil lamp. It was flickering and ready to go out. She rubbed her eyes and gazed outside to see Ruth trudging into the yard with a large sack of barley.

When she came in the house, a sleepy-eyed Naomi greeted her with a hug and a smile.

> And when she came to her mother in law, she said, Who art thou, my daughter? And she told her all that the man had done to her. And she said, These six measures of barley gave he me; for he said to me, Go not empty unto thy mother in law." (Ruth 3:16–17)

Ah, this is great, Naomi thought. *All went well last night. Thank you, Lord.* She gave Ruth further instructions.

> Then said she, Sit still, my daughter, until you know how the matter will fall: for the man will not be in rest, until he have finished the thing this day." (Ruth 3:18)

This was wise counsel coming from Naomi. She knew in her heart that this was a top priority for Boaz. He was a man of action and commitment. He would follow through on this until its conclusion. She advised Ruth to wait. Now, it was in the Lord's hands.

CHAPTER 7

Take Responsibility

Then went Boaz up to the gate, and sat him down there: and, behold, the kinsman of whom Boaz spake came by; unto whom he said, Ho, such a one! Turn aside, sit down here. And he turned aside, and sat down. And he took ten men of the elders of the city, and said, Sit ye down here, And they sat down. And he said unto the kinsman, Naomi, that is come again out of the country of Moab, selleth a parcel of land, which was our brother Elimelech's: And I thought to advertise thee, saying, Buy it before the inhabitants, and before the elders of my people. If thou wilt redeem it, redeem it: but if thou will not redeem it, then tell me, that I may know: for there is none to redeem it beside thee; and I am after thee. And he said, I will redeem it. (Ruth 4: 1-4)

The business of the city took place at the gate. This was a gathering place for community leaders. The elders fulfilled the roles of judges. Boaz arrived early and sat down where he could see all who came by the gate.

Within a short time, this close relative of his and Elimelech's came by. His name was not given. Boaz was not worried about the close relative agreeing to redeem the property, and without hesitation, he continued with the transaction.

> Then said Boaz, What day thou buyest the field of the hand of Naomi, thou must buy it also of Ruth the Moabitess, the wife of the dead, to raise up the name of the dead upon his inheritance." (Ruth 4:5)

Now Boaz gave him the rest of the obligation. If this relative redeemed the land of Elimelech, he would also have to redeem Ruth. Boaz revealed to him she was a Moabitess. Deuteronomy 23:3 forbade congregating with a Moabite, though marriage to a Moabite was not forbidden. The relative immediately declined this extra obligation. According to him, it would ruin the family inheritance plans. This was great news for Boaz. Boaz knew he was doing the bidding of the Lord's purposes, so he was not worried.

> And the kinsman said, I cannot redeem it for myself, lest I mar mine own inheritance:

> redeem thou my right to thyself; for I cannot redeem it." (Ruth 4:6)

This opened the door for Boaz to redeem Ruth.

> Now this was the manner in former time in Israel concerning redeeming and concerning changing, for to confirm all things; a man plucked off his shoe, and gave it to his neighbour: and this was a testimony in Israel. (Ruth 4:7)

The book of Ruth was written much later than these events. At the writing of this story, removing one's sandal was no longer the custom for a kinsman-redeemer. Evidently, if he took off his shoe and gave it to Boaz, it signified he would not walk on the land and was handing that right over to Boaz.

> Therefore the kinsman said to Boaz, Buy it for thee. So he drew off his shoe. And Boaz said unto the elders and unto all the people, Ye are witnesses this day, that I have bought all that was Elimelech's, and all that was Chilion's and Mahlon's, of the hand of Naomi. Moreover, Ruth the Moabitess, the widow of Mahlon, I

> have purchased to be my wife, to raise up the name of the dead upon his inheritance, that the name of the dead be not be cut off from among his brethren, and from the gate of his place: Ye are witnesses this day." (Ruth 4:8–10)

This was a commitment. Boaz was a man of his word. He was both confident and competent. He promptly and resolutely took care of business. What better person to take the role of a kinsman-redeemer than Boaz? He was half-Jew and represented the reconciliation of Jesus reaching out to the Gentiles for their redemption and salvation. Jesus was a kinsman-redeemer. Man needed a mediator (Jesus) between God and himself. Boaz epitomized the love and compassion of a redeemer, and his life showed the compassion of Jesus.

This was a wonderful day for Boaz. He had just made a lifelong commitment to support Ruth, Naomi, and any children he had with Ruth. He assumed the all-important role of protector and provider. He did not take this lightly. He counted the cost and did not complain about it. In fact, he took great pleasure in this role.

> And all the people that were in the gate, and the elders, said, We are witnesses. The Lord make the woman who is coming to thine house like Rachel and like Leah, which two did build the house of Israel; and do thou worthily in Ephratah, and be famous in Bethlehem: And let thy house be like the house of Pharez, whom Tamar bare unto Judah, of the seed which the Lord will give thee of this young woman." (Ruth 4:11–12)

Ephrathah was another name for a region of Bethlehem. In verse twelve, the elders were correctly linking Boaz to the house of Pharez (Perez), whom Tamar bore to the house of Judah. Boaz's father, Salmon, was descended from Tamar, and the elders knew it.

The Israelites fully accepted Ruth, even though she was a Moabitess. Her love and loyalty to Naomi in hard times revealed her true character to them. Boaz had now taken full financial responsibility for Ruth and Naomi. He was continuing a legacy that resulted in the line of David and ultimately led to Jesus. This was the beginning of a lifetime journey with Ruth, and the love story and redemption continued through the rest of their lives.

In the New Testament, we read what John the Baptist, Jesus's cousin, said about the threshing floor and one of Boaz and Ruth's descendants, Jesus. In Matthew 3:12, we read:

> Whose fan is in his hand, and he will throughly purge his floor, and gather his wheat into the garner; but he will burn up the chaff with unquenchable fire. (Matthew 3:12) (Garner is another word for barn or its equivalent).

These were the spoken words of John the Baptist as he described the beginning of Jesus's ministry. John the Baptist was talking about Jesus gathering up and securing His believers and at the same time dealing justice to those who rejected Him. John the Baptist talked about the activities of the threshing floor as an example many years after Boaz. The spiritual implications of Boaz and Ruth on the threshing floor represent Jesus's redemption of His followers.

Just like Jesus winnowed the wheat to secure His believers, Boaz winnowed the available women in

Bethlehem. No doubt parents who were interested in him becoming their son-in-law invited him many times for dinner or some other social occasion. They were chaff because God did not choose them. Boaz was close enough to God to know His will and waited for the best grain, Ruth, and found her waiting on his threshing floor. This was where they completed the deal for him to redeem her.

In the same way, the Lord takes great pleasure in redeeming us on the threshing floor of our lives. He wants to redeem us where we are at any time and in any condition. Sometimes people get winnowed and find themselves lying on the threshing floor seemingly helpless and do not know that the Lord looks at them as the best grain and is there to help them.

You build a lasting relationship in a marriage when you wait on the Lord and seek out the best grain available as your spouse. If you are close to God, He will show you what to do, just as he did for Ruth. You must be in the Word daily. If you are searching for a spouse, ask the Lord to sort through the chaff and give you spiritual discernment and wisdom in finding the good grain. A word of caution must be noted. Some people get into bad marriages and then claim that God told them it was the right person. They blame God for a bad choice. You must use common sense.

The wrong way to find a spouse is in the pages of Judges 14. Samson saw a Philistine woman in Timnah and told his father and mother to get her for him as a wife. Even though Samson was disobedient and reckless, the Lord used him for His purposes. (The Lord's purpose was to defeat the Philistines.) Samson used the eye gate instead of wisdom to find a wife. He allowed his fleshly appetite to control his behavior. The Philistine woman must have been beautiful, and that was all he considered in the transaction.

I believe the Lord has a sense of humor. He uses the most unlikely people to accomplish His purposes, and they often do so in strange ways. Samson may have been a mama's boy and a weakling at that. I suspect he did not look muscular like Victor Mature, who portrayed him in the movie *Samson*. I am just speculating, but he may have been thin and not muscular at all. He certainly surprised people with his God-given strength. And it *was* God who gave him his strength. Without God, he had no strength at all.

We know one thing, which is that his marriage was short lived. He ended up discarding his wife soon after the marriage. Seven days after the ceremony, she tricked him. She was then given to the best man at his wedding.

A wife needs to have her husband show his love for her. Samson clearly did not do this. He was immature and self-centered. He did not deserve a wife. He was not ready to love and nurture a woman. To him they were throwaway objects. A man typically acquires self-esteem from his occupational work and by providing for and protecting his family. He likes to receive assurances from his wife that he is living up to her expectations. If a man is spiritual leader in his home, his marriage and family life will be greatly enriched.

Boaz was a strong leader and was generous to others. His purpose was to glorify God by being a kinsman-redeemer, thereby fulfilling God's will for him. Men have an opportunity to glorify God by loving and appreciating their wives unconditionally.

If you look at the animal kingdom, many male animals must fight it out or prove themselves worthy for the privilege of mating. They compete for a scarce resource—a mate. Men today should have to prove themselves worthy of taking a woman for a wife, but they do not. Years ago, a young man had to talk to the girl's father and seek permission to date with honorable intentions. The father would look over the young man and test him on the elements of manhood—being a provider, protector, and spiritual leader. An attentive father did not want a young man with only animal instincts dating his daughter. This was part of preservation and protection for his daughter. Today, men do not have to prove themselves honorable. All they need to do is charm a girl into living with them and maybe marrying them later. This results in an unstable relationship that does not last. A man who can prove himself worthy is one who will be a candidate for an honorable lasting relationship.

Present-Day Marriage

There are men today who think their wives should pay their own way. I had a client come into my office one night without his wife. He wanted to file his taxes separate from her. I asked him if they had separated, and he replied that they had not. I then asked him why he wanted to file separately. He said she had worked a job and had no taxes withheld. He wanted her to pay her own taxes. I said to him, “Tell me, did your wife get the job to help out with the family finances?”

“Yes,” he timidly replied.

I then asked, “Did she cook you a nice dinner last night?”

He replied in the affirmative.

I continued, “Did you sleep with her last night?”

Again, he replied, “Yes.”

Then I asked him, “Do you want those last two things taken from you?”

“No,” he blurted out.

“Then you should be thanking her for all her work and help,” I said.

He hung his head and nodded in agreement. He simply had not thought about how his wife was trying to ease the financial burden for him.

Some men do not appreciate what their wives do for them. They do not think about how hard their wives work to preserve their family. Most women want a husband who will take control of his responsibility and show his loving care for them.

I taught at colleges and universities for several years. During that time, I observed a trend of fewer men attending college and taking the professional courses. Today, approximately 60 percent of the college entrants are women. Not all young men need to go to college. There are plenty of trades and occupations that do not require a college education. But increasing numbers of men are declining to take professional courses and a relying more on women to fill in the economic gap in their marriage.

Increasingly, young men are failing their role as protector and provider. They are alienating themselves from their God-given role of legitimate reproduction and manhood.

I also see increasingly that women who come into my office have better-paying jobs than their husbands. The men who do marry are marrying up in increasing numbers. Some of the young men practice serial monogamy. That is, they marry several times, never settling down with one wife. They do not seem to be interested in a long-term marriage. (There are also serial monogamy problems caused by women.)

Several clients have sons in their early twenties who do not hold a steady job or attend school. They just hang out at Mom and Dad's house with other young male friends all day and evening. Somehow, they missed out on learning their role in life. We need mentors and role models to guide these young men toward personal responsibility.

Marriage

It is important for couples contemplating marriage to sort out their expectations and make sure they are compatible. Besides other activities, I have a perfect premarital exercise for couples. It is to go canoeing together.

A couple of summers ago, we vacationed on Edisto Island in South Carolina. It was not my idea of a vacation destination, but my oldest daughter thought it would be a good adventure. One of the events she had planned for us was to all canoe from one small island to another. As my wife and I, with five decades of marriage, climbed into our canoe, it almost tipped over. I had to look at my watch, which has the word *relax* on its face. That was what I needed to do.

We each took a paddle and started canoeing. I tried to tell my wife what to do with her paddle, and next thing I knew, we were going in a circle. We then got stuck on a sand bar in the reeds. My wife thought it was funny and started laughing. I was less than amused. My goal was to get to the other island. Her goal was to have fun. We had a strong headwind, an incoming tide, and a lack of coordination, which made it difficult to advance. We ended up in the reeds a couple more times and landed on a sandbar each time. There were alligators in proximity, so I was not about to venture far out of the boat. We had a lot of dialogue, mostly negative, before we got to the other island.

With arms and backs aching, we finally hit shore, apologized to each other, and relaxed. The return trip was much easier. With the wind behind us and the tide pulling us in, the only problem we had was keeping the canoe straight. We ended up in the reeds a couple more times. By now, I found it humorous but had gained no confidence in my ability to navigate a two-person canoe. I took it as my responsibility to get us back to shore. We finally hit the return shore and climbed out, much relieved. This trip put many communication processes to the test. However, we were still talking to each other after this. Fortunately, we were able to pull together and see the humor in our experience.

Leadership

Part of taking responsibility is being a servant leader. Boaz was a servant leader. He made sure his employees had food, water, and rest during the long harvest hours. He served them by being there to experience what they were experiencing in the hard work. Boaz, in his leadership role, provided for the needs of his employees.

On this same trip to Edisto Island, we had another interesting experience. After we left the canoe landing, we came to a locked gate at the exit. *What else could happen?* I thought. We had two vehicles—my son's rental car and my own. We looked at the swamp on the right and left sides of the road. There was no way out but through the gate. I started looking around and found a faded phone number on the outer side of the gate. Even though we had poor reception, I called it out to my son, and he was able to phone the owner. The gate had a combination lock, and as the owner gave the combination, my son relayed the information to me. We finally got the gate opened and left. We still had more vehicles at the shore that had to exit, so we called them with the combination so they would not have the same issue. We had a problem and worked together to solve it.

Likewise, husbands and wives need to work together to solve problems that occur in their home. Along with this, by taking responsibility for his actions and leadership, a man learns skills and acquires character through the Lord's leading to shape the direction of his home.

CHAPTER 8

A Lifetime Journey

> So Boaz took Ruth and she was his wife: and when he went in unto her, the Lord gave her conception, and she bare a son. And the women said unto Naomi, Blessed be the Lord, which hath not left thee this day without a kinsman, that his name may be famous in Israel. And he shall be unto thee a restorer of thy life and a nourisher of thine old age: for thy daughter in law, which loveth thee, which is better to thee than seven sons, hath borne him." (Ruth 4:13–15)

The close relative mentioned in verse fourteen is Naomi's grandson. Although they were not blood relatives, he was still her legal grandson. This boy filled a void created when Naomi lost her husband and two sons. The Lord gave her a grandson. Children are a gift from the Lord.

> Lo, children are an heritage of the Lord.
>
> And the fruit of the womb is his reward.
>
> As arrows in the hand of a mighty man,

So are children of the youth.

Happy is the man that hath his quiver full of them:

they shall not be ashamed,

but they shall speak with the enemies in the gate.

(Psalm 127:3–5)

Her grandson no doubt played a key role in helping her during her old age. The gift of a grandson here is the beginning of Boaz and Ruth's legacy leading to their descendant Jesus, born several hundred years later. The neighbor women were so overwhelmed with the goodness of Ruth that they said she was better than having seven sons. This is a testimony to Ruth's caring for Naomi during difficult times.

And Naomi took the child and laid it on her bosom, and became nurse unto it. And the women her neighbors gave it a name, saying, There is a son born to Naomi;

and they called his name Obed: he is the father of Jesse, the father of David. (Ruth 4:16–17)

Obed means “one who serves.” This was appropriate in that he probably not only served the Lord, but he also served Naomi, Ruth, and Boaz as they got older and could not care for themselves. No doubt Boaz spent a lot of time with Obed. If he was like other fathers, then he would have taken Obed to the fields. He would have let him work there under his supervision. You could imagine Boaz standing up on the hill watching his son play in the fields, running back and forth through the barley stalks. Boaz would have taken the time to explain the whole farming process not only from a growing and harvesting standpoint, but also from an economic and spiritual perspective.

Given Boaz’s character, he would have shown an example of military service, headship in the home, and leadership in the community. Boaz was known in the gates and was highly respected by the community elders. Obed learned life skills from his father. Boaz also would have taught him the things of the Lord and provided a consistent example of what it meant to be a godly man. Obed was King David’s grandfather, and Boaz was King David’s great-grandfather.

Boaz's steady leadership provided stability in his family for generations. With the Lord's guidance, he would have been able to keep his commitment to his marriage and family, regardless of any interruptions.

During any marriage, a husband-and-wife relationship experiences tension, hurt feelings, anger, disappointment, and feelings of estrangement. Yes, it is possible that Boaz and Ruth experienced some of this during their marriage. They knew how to communicate, and Boaz specifically knew how to accept responsibility. Boaz knew that he did not have to prove he was right and win an argument. He was bigger than that. He knew how to submit all things to the Lord for direction.

> Husbands, love your wives, even as Christ also loved the church, and gave himself for it; that he might sanctify and cleanse it with the washing of water by the word, That he might present it to himself a glorious church, not having spot or wrinkle, or any such thing; but that it should be holy and without blemish. So ought men to love their wives as their own bodies. He that loveth his wife loveth himself. (Ephesians 5:25–28)

Men are accountable to the Lord for keeping a husband-and-wife relationship running smoothly. If a man does not love himself, do not marry him. If a marriage falls apart, men are oftentimes responsible for that outcome. There are exceptions, but a failed marriage could indicate that a husband was inattentive to his wife's needs. Men need to recognize their leadership role and bring the relationship back into balance when things go awry. Men honor God by maintaining a good relationship with their wives. When people talk about marital problems, they are essentially talking about a lordship problem. They are also talking about a leadership problem. This responsibility falls on the husband. He is to report to the Lord daily for instructions and to get his leadership instructions from God's Word.

A husband should start each day by thanking the Lord for his wife and acknowledging her as a gift. If he does, he is taking his leadership role seriously. A husband needs to consciously maintain a caring and loving attitude toward his wife. Couples who stay together do so because of a lifetime commitment. They do not let annoyances and inconveniences get in the way of their marriage. They know how to work out differences and communicate with each other effectively.

Boaz went into marriage fully willing to accept all the responsibilities of a husband. He knew this was a permanent relationship.

When sorting through the chaff and looking for the right mate, a person should understand that there are people of goodwill and those who are not. Both Boaz and Ruth were goodwilled persons.

There are times when my wife gets irritated with me. Usually, it starts with her saying something to me that I either did not hear or did not understand. At this point our communication has failed. I immediately do a self-check and affirm that she is a goodwilled person and harbors no ill will toward me or anyone else. Usually, when this happens, what one of us hears is not what the sender intended. Oftentimes, I do not hear the full sentence of what she is saying to me. This causes confusion. After much discussion, we eventually get it sorted out. I now make sure we are looking at each other when we are having a discussion.

The other day, I was sitting in our kitchen eating breakfast and noticed two doves sitting together on the fence. One dove was gently pecking the head of the other. The recipient was cooing as this act of affection took place. Doves mate for life. When they decide to mate, they make a lifetime commitment. Only death separates them. Later that week, I saw these doves building a nest on the inside eaves of my front porch. They flew in with pieces of straw and stem, one piece at a time, and gently placed them on the nest. Each dove was affectionate to the other. Married couples who show their love and affection for one another will build a deep and lasting bond, and a nest they can live in together for life.

When I was five years old, our family moved to a prairie house in Torrance, California, in the Los Angeles area. There was a large wooden oil derrick on the property. It pumped oil day and night, as did other derricks in that area. There were also small farms in the neighborhood. Right next door to us lived the Van Putts. Mr. Van Putt was a large, tall, muscular old man. As much as I could figure, he was born in the 1870s. He and his wife lived a meager existence and farmed off their land. One morning, I was astonished to see him tethered to a plow as he pulled it. His wife was behind the plow burrowing into the ground as he struggled to move the plow inch by inch. Occasionally, he would stop to see how his wife was doing and wipe the sweat from his brow with the gingham red bandana he kept in his pants pocket.

One day, after he finished working, my older brother Jim, and I went over to talk with him. Jim admired Mr. Van Putt's bantam chickens, and we talked about them for a while. We then went home and had dinner. Just as we were finishing our dessert of ice cream, Mr. Van Putt came knocking on the door. It was just before sundown, and he was standing there in his bib overalls with a red bandana hanging out of the right rear pocket, holding several bantam chickens for Jim. He said that he and his wife had decided Jim was ready to have his own brood of chickens. Straightaway, we took them to a makeshift shed and made sure they had a place to roost for the night. We left the shed door open for ventilation.

The next morning, we went out to check on the chickens and they were gone. Embarrassed, we went over to Mr. Van Putt's house and told him the chickens had disappeared. "I just wonder if ..." he said as we followed him to the barn. To our surprise, they had come home to roost in his barn's rafters. He apologized to us and said he would make sure we get some bantams that were not used to his barn. The next day, he delivered a brood of bantam chicks to our house from the feed store.

Mr. Van Putt was a man's man. He was a hard worker, loved his wife, was generous, and took time out for a couple of neighborhood boys. His actions were an inspiration to both of us. Later in life, each of us faced what seemed like impossible odds many times, and it helped us to persevere as we remembered the hard work and strong character of Mr. Van Putt.

One autumn morning, as the fog was clearing, I saw a black hearse at the back door of their house. Mr. Van Putt's lifetime journey was finished, but not his impact on others. Through his leadership and caring actions, he left a wonderful legacy for the wife of his youth and two young neighborhood boys.

CHAPTER 9

Family Legacy

And all thy children shall be taught of the Lord; and great shall be the peace of thy children.

—Isaiah 54:13

...but as for me and my house, we will serve the Lord.

—Joshua 24:15

How we raise our children, treat our spouses, and build our families will have an impact for generations to come. Right now, as I sit here, we have four living generations in our family. We are great-grandparents. Our son and his wife are grandparents. Our son's daughter is a mother, and her sons are our fourth generation of living relatives.

As I look at my family, the words of the apostle Paul in a letter to the believers at Philippi come to mind.

> I press toward the mark for the prize of the high calling of God in Christ Jesus. (Philippians 3:14)

Paul wanted to finish strong and glorify the Lord in all things. Our lives have a purpose, and we need to find it and pursue it. We who are parents have a very high calling and purpose in our children. As I look back, I wish I had spent more time mentoring my children and being with them. They were a high calling and a treasured purpose when under my watch. Instead of making a relationship with each of them a priority, I devoted my non-working hours to things I wanted to do for myself. I used to travel and make presentations, teach college several nights a week, and spend time in class preparation. These are all things that were temporary and had no lasting effect to my benefit. They consumed time I could have invested in furthering a relationship with my children.

How we influence our children is extremely important. If you are raising children, consider putting your personal desires and agenda on hold and focus on them and your spouse. After they are grown and gone, you will have plenty of time to fulfill these desires. Right now, being there for them, playing with them, taking them on fun outings and vacations, mentoring them, and instructing them in the Word are the important things to accomplish. This does not diminish the importance of the husband and father providing for his family. This is his life purpose.

No doubt, if Boaz lived to see Obed in his youth, he spent a lot of time with him. He understood what it took to make his family function. He probably had the opportunity to take Obed on walks and point out plants, scenery, crops, and animals and discuss anything that piqued Obed's curiosity.

You have a legacy to leave your descendants and need to be aware of the impact of your actions on their future. If you think you are being called to something, measure it against the backdrop of any children you have at home and your spouse. If you are in God's will, there will be no conflict with your decision regarding being called to something.

When I graduated with my master's degree in business, I interviewed with a prestigious consulting firm. One of the executives interviewed me and said that although I had an excellent background and work history, he was not going to hire me. He told me the job required long hours and a lot of travel, and it was not good for a father to be away from his children. He then said to check back with him in twenty years. He was right. Had I taken the job, I would have been an absentee father. I would have missed the important things that were going on in my children's lives.

As a postscript to this, I did take a consulting job about thirteen years later. My youngest child was in the sixth grade. This executive was right, as I found myself flying out on Sunday afternoons and returning on Friday nights. My wife would pick me up at the airport on Friday night and take me to my office so I could prepare reports and sort through all the things on my desk. Finally, at 2:00 a.m. on Saturday, I finished, and we headed to an all-night restaurant to have an early breakfast. Afterward, we went home. I slept until late morning. Around noon, I was ready to spend a couple of hours with my sixth grader. In one year, I travelled to twenty-six states and six countries. During this time, I missed out on my daughter's birthday celebration, school events, church events, and countless opportunities just to be with her.

After a year and a half, I was transferred to a local office that had minimal travel. This allowed the opportunity to do what Boaz did for Obed, that is to provide, protect, lead, and spend time with my daughter. Still, I lost a year and a half of quality time with her.

You may ask yourself, "What do I want written on my tombstone?" What is the legacy you want to leave for your family? We need to be available for God's calling. In Genesis 12:1, God called Abram, later named Abraham, and gave him an assignment. The Lord can call you at any time in your life and, through His call, bring you unexpected fulfillment. He will not call you for His purpose if it violates your parental responsibilities. You will not always know or realize the legacy you leave behind for others as you take your assignment from the Lord. Our goal should be to glorify our Lord.

I grew up in a home of two parents and five children. We had a fourteen-year gap between the oldest and the youngest. My older brother, Jim, was the first, and then I came along three years later. He and I were very close. He is now with our Lord and savior. Our father worked as a machinist in a factory. For several years, we lived in a modest, one-story, 1,250-square-foot, three-bedroom home with two bathrooms. Our father was a hard worker and provided the basic needs for his family. He insisted that Jim and I work jobs and start businesses.

Dad was not interested in attending church, but he made Jim and me go to Sunday school as soon as we could walk. Fortunately, he had us attend Bible-believing churches with a strong emphasis on children learning the Scriptures. When I was five years old, Jim and I rode our bicycles one and half miles from our prairie house to our downtown church. Occasionally, Dad would take us to church, drop us off, and go into town a few blocks away to Vurp's café and bar lounge.

On those days, his Sunday services consisted of imbibing several glasses of beer and interacting with the bartender and fellow bar patrons. On his way to pick us up from church, he stopped at a liquor store and purchased a six-pack of beer to drink while he was waiting for us at the church. As soon as I heard a beer can hitting the pavement, I knew Dad had arrived. He parked in the alley behind the Sunday school building. Jim and I knew where to find him.

"Learn anything today?" Dad inquired.

"We learned about Elijah killing a bunch of Ahab's prophets and then running away. God had the ravens feed him," I replied.

"Uh," he mumbled as he burped. Another can hit the pavement, the big Packard roared to life, and we headed home. He was interested in what we learned, but never took the discussion beyond what we told him.

Most Sunday afternoons, Jim and I rode our bicycles downtown to the matinee movie theater. My Sunday school teacher, a young man in his twenties, told us to stay away from movie theaters because they were evil. I ignored him because I saw nothing bad in the cartoons and Westerns I watched. One Sunday afternoon, Jim and I sat near the front of the theater eating popcorn as we watched other kids flatten their popcorn cartons and sail them toward the screen. This was pre-movie entertainment.

"Lenny, stop throwing cartons at the screen!" a familiar voice shouted. I looked up, and there was my Sunday school teacher. To my surprise, he worked at the theater he told us to avoid. His accusation that I was throwing things was not true. It bothered me that he worked at the theater. It did not make sense that he told me not to go to the movies but worked there. I thought he was dishonest. However, I was strong enough in the Bible stories I had read and heard to realize he was just human and had his failings. I also harbored some guilt because there were times I sat up in the loge and lobbed bonbons onto moviegoers below once the lights were out.

When I became a teenager, my brother Jim and I attended church instead of Sunday school. One Sunday morning, I noticed a sharp-dressed and well-groomed man in his twenties sitting in front of us. Jim leaned over and told me this guy was a second lieutenant in the army and had just graduated from West Point. My older brother always seemed to know everything.

This young lieutenant was a missile officer at Fort MacArthur in San Pedro, California. We saw him there every Sunday for several months. Decades later, I talked with our former associate pastor and asked him if he knew what had happened to that young officer. With fondness, the old pastor told us what happened to him. This young officer met a young woman and married her in the same church. The men in his platoon were so fond of him they brought a Nike missile on a large army flatbed trailer to the wedding as tribute to his leadership. They had the base commander's approval. The old pastor said that shortly thereafter, the young officer volunteered for Army Special Forces and went to Fort Bragg, North Carolina, for a year of training. After he graduated, the army sent him to South Vietnam. This was in the early 1960s, and by then, he had two young daughters and left them and his wife behind as he went off to war. He was a godly man and a wonderful leader to his men.

One night, the North Vietnamese overran their small outpost. They killed this young officer while he was defending his men. Months later, his widow received a small package in the mail from one of his former soldiers. The soldier had written her a letter and included a bloodstained Gideon New Testament in the package. The soldier wrote that her husband had used this testament to lead devotions and inspire his men in the jungle far away from civilization and during most difficult and hostile times. The North Vietnamese soldier who had killed her husband unbuttoned the shirt pocket on his lifeless body and took the testament. The soldier writing the letter said he later killed that North Vietnamese soldier in a firefight and found the testament in his possession. He said he recognized it and wanted her to have it along with a testimony as to how wonderful a leader and how godly a man he was.

This young officer gave his all. He glorified God by his example. He led devotions and encouraged his men in the things of the Lord. His men will never forget him. His legacy lives on.

Boaz and Ruth left a legacy for generations to follow. Jesus was born in Bethlehem, where Boaz and Ruth married and raised Obed. They had no idea of their legacy of Jesus as a descendant several hundred years later.

The complete book of Ruth was probably written sometime after the events of Boaz and Ruth. We know this is because we see the lineage from Obed to Jesse to David at the end of Ruth.

> Now these are the generations of Pharez (Perez): Pharez begot Hezron, Hezron begat Ram, and Ram begat Amminadab, And Amminadab begot Nahshon, And Nahshon begat Salmon, And Salmon begot Boaz, and Boaz begat Obed, And Obed begot Jesse, and Jesse begat David. (Ruth 4:18–22)

CHAPTER 10

Called for His Purpose

The Lord uses unlikely persons to accomplish His purposes. Rahab, Boaz's mother, is a good example. She was a brave woman and helped the children of Israel to conquer Jericho. In Joshua 2:1–21 and 6:22–23, we read about her part of the conquering of Jericho, where Joshua sent two spies. They were to go in without being detected, survey the strengths and weaknesses of the city, map out the main paths, and make an overall assessment on the feasibility of conquering it. They entered the city in the dark of night, but someone saw them.

Imagine them walking down a narrow road with dogs barking and bright moonlight shining on them. They searched for and found Rahab, who was an innkeeper and harlot. They quietly went up to her inn and knocked, and she let them in. They stayed there for several hours obtaining important information.

The Lord orchestrated their meeting with Rahab. God knew that in her line of business, she could provide valuable information to them. In addition, God wanted her to connect with the Israelites. Rahab was well known in town and regarded by the king as a source of information. It was no surprise that when the king heard from his intelligence staff that two Israelites had come into town, he immediately sent messengers to Rahab's inn to find out where they were.

She would be the first to know if anyone new came into town. However, the spies were under the Lord's protection. The king's messengers came to the inn and started banging on the door. Rahab confidently opened the door and took control of the situation. She told the messengers the spies had come but departed just as the gate was closing for the night. The king's men believed her, quickly departed, and pursued the men in the wrong direction given them by Rahab.

Rahab shared her belief in God with the spies. She told them that she knew the Lord had given them the land and that she had heard the story about the water being held back and the pathway drying up in the Red Sea. She then acknowledged God was in heaven above and on earth beneath. She believed in the Lord.

Rahab promised to continue to help them. They told her she and her family would be spared for helping them. She was told that if she hung a scarlet cord out of her window, her family inside the inn would be safe during the invasion. She told the spies to go to the mountain and stay there for three days and they would be safe. What she did required bravery. She had to remain cool under pressure. The king would have executed Rahab if he had found out the truth of her shielding these men. Her faith in God gave her the opportunity to exhibit this incredible bravery.

After Jericho fell, Rahab and her family were brought out and stayed with the Israelites. Not long after this, Salmon discovered Rahab and married her. She was Boaz's mother.

Rahab is an example of how the Lord can call anyone to serve Him. It does not matter what kind of baggage you have in your past. The Lord can cleanse you, forgive you, honor you, and call you for His purposes.

When Rahab heard about how great God was, she believed in Him and surrendered her all to Him. She risked her life and that of her family by protecting the two spies who came to visit her. The Lord honored her by putting her in the direct line of Christ.

Rahab, being Boaz's mother, would have greatly influenced him during his formative years. She and Salmon instilled a strong work ethic, responsibility, leadership, management, and compassion into Boaz. They also influenced Boaz through their strong belief in the Lord and made sure their actions reflected this belief. Rahab helped him to become all that a man should be. They both get credit for raising Boaz to be such a great person in the community. He took all the things he learned from Rahab and Salmon and instilled them into the character of his son Obed. He passed the baton of good things on to him.

Let's go down three generations to Solomon's birth. His parents were King David and Bathsheba. The story is recorded in 2 Samuel chapters 11–12. David unjustly took Bathsheba as his wife after he had her husband, Uriah, killed. Their first child died. Then she bore Solomon. He was God's choice. Even though wrong was committed by David and Bathsheba, the Lord used Bathsheba to bear a child who would be in the line of Christ.

Another twenty-four generations later, we reach Mary, the mother of Jesus. In Luke 1, the angel Gabriel comes to Mary and tells her that she would become the mother of Jesus. Mary was barely in her teens, a virgin, and was engaged to Joseph. Mary's last recorded response was in verse thirty-eight: "And Mary said, Behold the handmaid of the Lord; be it unto me according to thy word. And the angel departed from her." This response suggests that she was humble and willing to serve and obey the Lord. She surrendered all to Him.

Luke 1:46–55 is Mary's hymn. She recounts what the Lord has done for her in His great plan and for others preceding her.

This hymn in Latin has been called the "Magnificat" (Latin for "magnifies").

> "And Mary said, My soul doth magnify the Lord.
>
> And my spirit hath rejoiced in God my Saviour.
>
> For he hath regarded the low estate of his handmaiden:
>
> For, behold, from henceforth all generations shall call me blessed.

For he that is mighty hath done to me great things;

and holy is his name.

And his mercy is on them that fear him from generation to generation.

He hath shewed strength with his army;

He hath scattered the proud in the imagination of their hearts.

He hath put down the mighty from their seats,

And exalted them of low degree.

He hath filled the hungry with good things;

And the rich he hath sent empty away.

He hath holpen his servant Israel,

In remembrance of his mercy;

As he spake to our fathers,

to Abraham, and to his seed for ever."

Holpen is old English for help.

The psalms of David referred to David's vertical relationship with God. Many generations later, Mary extolled in a hymn how great our God is and what He has done for us. If we look at Rahab, Ruth, and Mary, collectively, we see a common thread that resulted in total surrender to God. God called each of them to duty, and they reported to Him as their commander and courageously served Him.

When a man and woman marry, they are called for a purpose. It is not an accident that men and women fall in love, get married, and have children. The Lord has a purpose for each of us. Getting married is the first step in building a family legacy. If we surrender, the Lord will direct our steps and find a compatible mate for us. (His will for some is that they remain single or childless and he has a purpose for them). I can see the hand of the Lord guiding me when I was a teenager. I found my future wife in a bookkeeping class. After we married, the Lord guided us to teaching the Bible to young people. We began with teaching Sunday school.

If we submit to his will, the Lord will give us direction on His purpose for our lives. If He calls us, then He will equip us for the task. He doesn't call you to do something without equipping you. We must be open to learning and listening.

In a marriage, we combine two self-interests with eternal purposes. Corporately, a couple needs to sort out direction from the Lord so that they go in the same direction. This requires prayer and a lot of talking.

Marriage is an institution that should grow and mature with each passing year. An ideal outcome is an agreement between a married couple on direction and the emphasis of eternal purposes in a mature marriage.

Young couples will find it beneficial if they concentrate on building a strong, Christ-centered marriage and emphasize this commitment when they have children. This is a priority calling for child-rearing couples and other couples. Our young people today are confused and in many instances without direction. They see the world differently from their parents. A family that devotes its emphasis to eternal things will have better direction than unbelieving individuals. Young people desperately need direction.

Emphasis on our calling has different stages due to our family situations. Newly married couples have a different calling than older couples who may be retired. These various stages are outlined below.

The priority for serving the Lord has its stages in life:

Stage	**Purpose**
Engagement	Sort out agreed eternal values.
Early marriage	Build a strong, Christ-centered marriage.
Child-rearing years	Instill biblical principles in children.
Post-child-rearing	Mentor descendants and serve in areas of eternal purposes.
Retirement	Serve the Lord to one's fullest ability and finish strong.
No longer here	Your legacy of example and instruction continues.

A husband's life calling is to provide for and protect his family. He is the spiritual leader. A married woman's primary life purpose is to invest in eternal purposes which includes helping her husband and mentoring her children.

Engaged Couples

Many years ago, I taught a personal finances segment in a premarital counseling series at our church. The goal of the series was to help young, engaged couples to sort out expectations, values, compatibility, communication, child-rearing values, and knowledge of one another. This series caused more than a few couples to reevaluate their relationship and their plans for marriage. I asked them to prepare a budget and discuss financial control. Agreeing on finances was one of the most difficult issues for them to sort out. This is where we had the highest drop-out rate. Some couples could not agree on how to manage their finances once they are married. There are several references in the Bible regarding money, and I used them as a basis for discussion.

We found that in many cases, at the beginning of the series, the couples were not facing the reality of the consequences of marriage. Some couples had not thought about basic living responsibilities and needed to confront those issues before marriage. This confirmed the need for engaged couples to discover and work through unresolved issues before they get married. The ones who were successful built a strong basis for their relationship.

Newly Married Couples

Couples face the reality of living together when they get married. If they have gone through premarital counseling and talk over life issues outside of counseling often, they should experience minimal behavioral surprises. Newly married couples obviously include young, never married couples; older and never married couples; previously married couples; and couples where one partner has never married and the other has. Each experiences a different dynamic. The common thread is to build a Christ-centered marriage. It is important to set aside time each day to pray and read the Bible together. I find that first thing in the morning with coffee and the evening near bedtime are best for us. This relaxed time allows us to focus on instructions from the Lord. Praying together solidifies our close relationship as a couple.

Child-Rearing Years

When children come along, family prayer is important. We always made sure one or both of us prayed with our children before they went to bed. We also set aside one evening each week for family devotions.

Previously married couples may have a more complicated relationship if there are children in the home from a previous marriage(s), and continuing communication with possible conflict concerning ex-spouses. I remember one couple in our premarital series who had difficulty deciding what role the husband would have in raising his future wife's ten-year-old son from a previous marriage. They were far along in their relationship and had set a date, but this lingering issue came up as unresolved during counseling. The man wanted a role in raising the son, including mentoring and discipline. The mother wanted the stepfather to have no role in raising the child. Wisely, they decided not to get married.

Raising children is a high purpose for couples. Children are a gift from the Lord. He has a purpose for each child and entrusts children to us for instruction, nurturing, and spiritual guidance. Couples who focus on their marriage and children will experience a meaningful family.

Post-Childrearing

My wife and I raised three children. When our son graduated from high school, he left home and joined the Army. Our home life immediately changed. It was difficult to let go of our son. I sat down one morning at breakfast and found it hard to talk about his leaving the home. He grew up too soon. Just about the time I had adjusted to his departure, it was time for our oldest daughter to go to college. After she left home, I can remember being in the attic looking for something and I came across a crop and a rope she had used when riding a pony as a little girl. I welled up with emotion. All the memories of her riding and the excitement of taking her on the trail and to the riding ring came back in a flash. (We recently lost this daughter to cancer. We have the confidence of her eternal salvation with our Lord and Savior and look forward to seeing her in heaven). I had similar feelings when our last child left home. They all grew up too soon. Our house became quiet after our last daughter left. Eventually, our barnyard animals either died or were given away, and

Lynn and I found ourselves much like newlyweds again. It was just us two in the home. This was an opportunity for us to strengthen our marriage by spending more time with each other. We seized the opportunity to spend more time serving the Lord.

We developed a corporate purpose, and it is teaching the Bible to children. My wife is a volunteer director for after-school Bible clubs. She manages over one hundred volunteers, provides teacher training, and teaches one or two clubs. This is more than a full-time commitment. My role is to provide administrative, financial, and logistical support. Additionally, I devote at least two Sunday mornings a month participating in a chapel program outreach to U.S. Marine Corps recruits during their last four weeks of training. I pray with them and teach a spiritual fitness class to them. My specialty is Old Testament battles and the apostle Paul's weapons of warfare from Ephesians 6. I relate these battles to our personal battles and provide application from God's word from Ephesians 6 to help them. Thankfully six decades ago I went through the Marine Corps NCO academy and have this in my background so I can relate to what they are experiencing.

The focus of our senior years is to serve and glorify God. The takeaway here is to spend your senior years doing something productive for the Lord.

Retirement

Some people decide not to retire and keep busy with an occupation or profession. Years ago, I taught an income tax class in Richmond, Virginia. One of the attendees wore a hat that set him apart from other attendees. Inscribed on his hat were "WWII," "Korea," and "Vietnam." I introduced myself and asked him about his military service. He told me he was eighteen when he fought in the Battle of the Bulge. Then, when the Korean War broke out, he was sent into combat once again. Because he was a staff sergeant and showed a strong military bearing, the army gave him a direct officer's commission. He went on to serve in combat in Vietnam. He retired after serving thirty-five years in the Army. Instead of retiring, he studied at a university and received a master's degree in taxation. He told me he was eighty-eight years old and did not plan on retiring. Some people retire only when they are no longer able to perform their duties.

For those who choose retirement, there is a wide range of opportunities for keeping busy. Some choose to travel, others volunteer their time, and some do a little of each and find time for family. There is a vast opportunity for persons who retire to serve others. Many ministries would love to have their help. When a person retires, he or she does not have to give up on life's meaningful purposes. That person can open a new chapter in life by enjoying a variety of things while still being useful.

No Longer Here

This may seem like a strange heading to consider, but it is here for a reason. When we pass away, people who lived during our time will remember us. They may not think of us all the time, but memories of our interaction will be there. Our descendants will have stories to tell about us. They record what we say and do in their memory. What do we want said about us? This is our challenge. Will our families remember us as fair, friendly, kind, and honorable? Will they credit us for guiding them in the right direction? Will we leave a spiritual legacy? Will they have fond memories of vacations, outings, and other recreation? Will they say we invested time in their lives? Will they say we mentored them? It is never too late to get engaged with your descendants. Let them experience good things with you.

CHAPTER 11

A Strong Marriage

> That the aged men be sober, grave, temperate, sound in faith, in charity, in patience. The aged women likewise that they be in behaviour as becometh holiness, not false accusers, not given to much wine, teacher of good things; that they may teach the young women to be sober, to love their husbands, to love their children; to be discreet, chaste, keepers at home, good, obedient to their own husbands, that the word of God be not blasphemed. Young men likewise exhort to be sober minded.
>
> —Titus 2:2–6

If you are married or contemplating marriage, you need to look at it as a lifetime commitment. Marriage is not an institution of convenience. It requires unconditional love for your spouse even during difficult times. Marriage requires an ongoing maintenance. Married couples need to keep the flame of love going by continuing to do things together that enrich their marriage.

I have clients who are widowed. Even though their spouses have passed away, they still have a deep love and affection for their memories.

Years ago, Jerry Livingston and Paul Francis Webster wrote a song, and Johnny Mathis sang it. The title is "The Twelfth of Never."

It mentions that roses need rain to sustain life. The singer needs showers of love from his lover to keep going. This is a life-sustaining statement. The life of a marriage requires nurturing and stimulation to remain healthy. Husbands and wives need to discover things they can do to continually nurture the relationship.

This song gives examples of a person's infinite love for another. Each of the following events described is in an impossibility. With these impossibilities, the singer tells how he feels about the forever relationship. The impossibilities are that bluebells would forget to bloom, clover would lose its perfume, poets would run out of rhyme, and he would stop loving and needing her.

Bluebells represent what you see in a marriage. The bluebell is a beautiful flower with its bright color. We need to see the beauty in our spouses and in the marriage itself.

There is an aroma in clover that leaves a feeling of familiarity and simple elation. The olfactory impression is pleasant. Our love for our spouses needs to leave a sweet scent in the relationship where we build up each other. We should be pleasant to our spouse.

This song has a poetic rhyme to it. If a husband and wife are in the right relationship, they will continue to rhyme and not have discord as they complement each other. In relationships, it is important to show our love for our spouse as a never-ending endearment, even during difficult times.

In the teen years of my marriage, I came up with my own example, and on occasion, I share it with my wife. I tell her to imagine an eagle flying by the earth every ten thousand years and brushing it with its wing. The time it would take the eagle to pare down the earth to nothing is only the beginning of my love for her. This may seem silly, but it is my way of affirming to my wife that our relationship is forever. This example provides a sense of stability to her. I am in this marriage for a long, long time. As of this writing it is sixty years and keeps getting stronger and better.

Music plays a key part in fostering a love relationship. If taken to heart, it can help a marriage last a lifetime. It provides a backdrop in sharing our feelings with one another.

During my more than six decades of marriage, I have accumulated some thoughts and observations on why it has lasted. It was not easy, especially in the early years. We discovered early in the marriage that it was important for us to be committed to preserving our love for each other, even during difficult times with our relationship. We had to diligently pursue keeping our marriage alive and healthy. I have a list of things for the husband, for the wife, and for both that may be helpful in accomplishing a long-lived marriage. My wife, Lynn, supplied some of these suggestions. You may already be practicing these things.

Husband

1. Every day, acknowledge that your wife is a gift from the Lord. Thank the Lord for her. Tell her that you appreciate and love her. Do the same for your children. Be generous with hugs and affirmation to all your family members.
2. Randomly surprise her with flowers or a similar acknowledgement.
3. If you have not already done so, set aside a weekly date night, if possible. Let her know you are still courting her.
4. Open the door for her when she enters and exits the car. Look at her and smile in admiration. If you do not admire her, pray for healing in your marriage.
5. Ask her how you can help her. I know this could take you away from your agenda, but it is worth it. You are a team. If it looks like she needs help, then get right in there and help her. Take on a gung-ho spirit of working together.
6. Get into the habit of clearing off the table after a meal. Put away food, bus the dishes, and generally get things in order. I only started this after thirty-two years of marriage. I am a slow learner. It took my wife being in a wheelchair

for a year from a head on auto crash for me to learn that I need to help in the kitchen. I also learned how to do laundry, iron, and fold clothes.

7. Write short notes of encouragement to your wife.
8. Listen to her. To be effective, this requires face-to-face interaction.
9. Please remember her birthday and anniversary. It is an honor to your wife to recognize your anniversary. Make it a special occasion.
10. Only look at your wife. I know. You are somewhere in public and the hottest thing you ever saw walks toward you, and you automatically look at her. Do not look a second time. It is embarrassing and deprecating to your wife for you to ogle another woman. It also hurts her feelings and creates insecurity. Finally, lusting is not good for your spiritual health.
11. If you are not already, then become the spiritual leader in your home. If you have neglected it for a long time, start now and assert what the Lord has ordained you to do. There are plenty of daily devotionals out there.

If you do not know anything about the Bible, get in there and start reading. Get into a verse-by-verse Bible study. The Lord will guide you. If you have children in the home, you will be a blessing by reading the Bible to them and leading them in prayer. I used to like reading stories out of the Bible to my children. Now, at night, during the last thirty minutes before lights-out, I read a portion of Scripture and a few pages out of a Christian book to my wife. Usually, I can only get through a couple of pages. Then we have prayer and it is lights-out. Pray with your wife and children. Participate in saying goodnight to your children and tucking them in with a prayer. You have a limited number of years to tuck in your children. They grow up quickly.

12. Exercise discipline without anger. Some parents believe in corporal punishment, or spanking. I personally think it should end when a child reaches eleven or twelve years of age. You should never strike a child with your hand. When our children were young and they needed a swat, we used an old Vans tennis

shoe. The child got wacked on the rear. We made sure this was not done in anger. We always talked about the infraction first, and then the swat followed. A hug and reassuring affirmation followed the swat.

13. Do not let the sun go down on your wrath. Lynn and I decided early in our marriage to settle our accounts before the lights went out for the night. If we had an outstanding issue, then we needed to discuss and resolve it before bedtime. I can tell you—sometimes it was not easy. Ill feelings and hurts are difficult to overcome, especially if you are tired or exhausted.

14. You do not have to win an argument. I have found many times that pursuing a disagreement was not worth the discord. It is sometimes better to let the issue drop so that you don't head toward an escalating argument.

15. Recognize your manly strength. You are most likely physically stronger than your wife. This requires tender responsibility. Do not abuse your God-given physical strength. A man is not

to physically bully his wife. Your wife depends on you for protection and provision. That is why you are physically stronger.

16. You are the priest in your home. With this comes the responsibility for setting the mood of the household. Your language and actions influence behavior. Your children will copy what you say and do. Words of encouragement rather than name-calling set the stage for a warm, loving home. You are the leader and chief encourager. Your wife and children depend on your leadership.

17. You and your wife should jointly agree on large decisions. There have been times when my wife and I did not agree on a purchase and walked away from it. We set it up as a protection from making foolish decisions. Each of us has veto power. There were a few times when I overruled Lynn's wise counsel. Unfortunately, I ended up suffering the natural consequences of a bad decision. Once made without her agreement, I owned my choice. It was my job to live with that solo decision. A bad decision

today is a down payment on tomorrow's problems.

18. Report to the Lord as your commander daily. Ask Him to give you a kingdom view of all your transactions. Ask the Lord to direct your steps and give you wisdom as you go about your day. Read Proverbs often.

19. Give your best to your employer, clients, or customers. Avoid complaining. Try to see the Lord's work in all you experience, even when others are unfair to you.

20. Your wife gets some of her self-esteem from your affirmation of her. Encourage, praise, and honor her often.

21. If your wife has a job outside of the home, give her special consideration by helping her and listening to her discussions about the workplace. She will need your helping hand if she put in a long day. Both of you may be tired but give her top priority and do what is needed to relieve her from stress.

Wife

1. The wife is the most powerful person in the household. Your influence is greater than your husband's. Women have a special position in the family. Remember this when things are not going well for you. Family members will sometimes neglect to tell you how much you are appreciated.
2. Encourage your husband in his pursuits toward self-improvement.
3. Caution your husband when you are not comfortable with what he is doing.
4. Be confident in your womanly intuition and thought process that is protective of the home.
5. Your prayers and attention to each family member and household event is important throughout your long day.

6. Men get their self-esteem from their work. Be sensitive to a bad day. Listen to your husband's complaints and encourage him. I went through a horrible time with one employer, and each day as I left for work, my wife would remind me that I was on assignment from the Lord. She also slipped notes into my attaché case that told me to have a good

day. This encouraged me to do my best and to maintain a kingdom view of interactions throughout the day. When I came home, she had the spa heated up and handed me swim trunks and a towel. More than forty years ago, my wife purchased a greeting card with a caricature of a smiling lion dressed as an aviator leaning on his biplane wing. Inside, the card read, "Have a good day, Ace." She photocopied it many times over the years and added Scripture and words of encouragement to me when I was about to take a trip or exam or have an interview or anything else that was important. I still have the original card and treasure it as an ongoing encouragement from my wife.

7. The wife can set the mood in the household. Discover ways to make each mealtime pleasant and relationship enriching. We had a rule in our home: no TV and/or other distractions, including nonemergency phone calls, during meals. Sometimes we had a whisper of pleasant music in the background. We made sure we had a table where we could all sit together and talk face-to-face. Oh, yes, there were times when issues were brought up during dinner that resulted in an

unpleasant meal for all. But mealtime is not for combat. Try to minimize this kind of interaction. It is better to take up issues outside of mealtime. If you have children, you want them to have fond memories of eating together as a family. Encourage your husband to be spiritual leader. His leadership can make family meals pleasant and generate lasting, affirming memories.

8. Avoid nagging. As your marriage progresses, there will be plenty of things that stack up as unpleasant to you about your husband. Your husband may spend too much time by looking at his electronic device, watching sports and TV in general, and pursuing time wasting activities. He may have gained too much weight and have a big belly. He may not be involved with the children enough. He may not be the spiritual leader and by default relegate it to you. Ask the Lord to give you wisdom on how to approach each issue. Encourage husband to be more productive if he has morphed into a lazy person. Share your concern with him that he may be wasting his life. Pray for him. If he is overweight, cook him healthy meals and encourage him to lose weight for health reasons. Tell him you want him

around for a long time. My wife recently gave me a handout received in the mail from a weight loss organization. The heading read, "Why I Want to Lose Weight." The lined page was blank, to be filled in by a person who wants to lose weight. I immediately thought of three reasons: I may live longer, look better, and feel better. Ask your husband if he would like to participate in a Bible reading with you and the children. Try to make it fun. Take turns telling Bible stories. Tell him you respect his leadership position and would like to see him lead the family in the things of the Lord. Small things, such as him squeezing the neck of a toothpaste tube, throwing towels on the floor with his discarded clothes, or forgetting to turn off lights are not worth a fight. They are annoyances but nonessentials.

9. Don't use sex as a weapon by withholding it from your husband when you are mad at him. This creates an untenable relationship and is dangerous to your marriage.
10. Help your husband when he is vulnerable. Twice I have asked my wife to bring an extra set of car keys to my location because I was locked out. The first

time, I locked myself out of the car just before teaching a university class, and my books and papers were in inside the car. Fortunately, I was early, and my wife was available. She immediately drove thirty-five miles to the university and saved the day for me. I normally have an extra set of keys under the bumper, but they must have fallen off. The second time was when I was more than sixty miles away. I had spare keys under the bumper but no key for the steering wheel lock device. This time I had two hours before class.

My wife is constantly looking out for me. It ranges from small grooming issues to health concerns. I have been able to return the favor over the years. Once, she was having lunch with friends and gave me a call for help. She had left her money at home and needed cash to pay for her lunch. I was available and quickly drove to the restaurant. I walked in, greeted her friends, and coolly and inconspicuously gave her the cash she needed. I was glad to do it and never said anything about it afterward.

Both

1. Work together on your finances and budget. Sort out needs from wants. A successful marriage depends on both of you agreeing on how to handle the money entrusted to you by the Lord. God owns it all, and you are both trustees of the money the Lord provides.
2. If you have children, spend as much time as possible with them. Pray about any opportunities that would take your time away from them.
3. Initiate marriage maintenance. Get alone and have fun together. Write notes to each other exuding encouragement, thankfulness, and appreciation.
4. Express your love for one another. Kissing, embracing, touching, and offering kind words and unrequested help are just a few of the things than can spark a marriage. Sincerely affirm each other daily. Showing affection keeps a marriage going.
5. Concentrate on building a marriage mansion. There is nothing wrong with building a large house and having abundant material possessions, but a top priority is building a marriage with large rooms filled with love, consideration, affection, understanding, help, encouragement, worship of our Lord,

togetherness, recreation, date nights, fun, selflessness, giving, and family.

CHAPTER 12
Passing the Baton

> Therefore shall ye lay up these my words in your heart and in your soul, and bind them for a sign upon your hand, that they may be as frontlets between your eyes. And ye shall teach them your children, speaking of them when thou sittest in thine house, and when thou walkest by the way, when thou liest down, and when thou risest up. And thou shalt write them upon the door posts of thine house, and upon thy gates.
>
> —Deuteronomy 11:18–20

When we date, become engaged, get married, and raise children, we do not know what the future is for our family's succeeding generations. Boaz and Ruth had no idea that several hundred years later in the same town, Jesus, the Messiah, and their descendant, would be born and be a kinsman-redeemer for all who would ask for salvation, repent, and believe. Their successive generations passed the baton of a true belief in God, our Lord, for this to be preserved. As you ponder this, pray for your descendants.

When we have children, we are responsible for shaping their lives and preparing them for adulthood. This is a deep responsibility. When our first child was born, I had just turned twenty-one. My wife and I were given the responsibility to raise our son. We learned parenting as he grew. Later, we had two more children. We have our list of regrets. Had we known better, there are things we would have done differently. This happens to all parents as they look back. We tried our best and attended seminars and classes on parenting during our child-rearing years. By God's grace, our children all turned out to be responsible, God-fearing citizens.

There is one thing I would change for sure if I were given another opportunity to parent. I would spend less time on my agenda and more time with my children. The focused time you spend with your children will reap great rewards for you and them. I am talking about time where you mentor them, spend time with them, help them, teach them, affirm them, lovingly correct them, and show an interest in them. Thankfully, I learned you should not punish your children, but discipline them.

Disciplining a child gives him or her an opportunity to correct behavior. Discipline is like the banks of a river. Just as riverbanks guide the water, discipline can guide behavior. We need to guide our children rather than revile them. Show them the benefits of doing what is right.

Parents should faithfully tuck in their children with a prayer each night before they go to bed. I wish I could recapture the missed opportunities when other priorities replaced those important moments.

What creates a home where you can pass on good memories? I once read of a family of several siblings who kept the family farm for many years after their parents died. The children finally decided they needed to tear down the empty, dilapidated house. They waited until the weather was pleasant and chose a Saturday. They all showed up with tools and started tearing apart the house. When they came to the living room, each of them thought of an excuse why they were done for the day. Some were shedding tears. They gathered their tools and left the farm. None of them returned to finish the job. Later, as they discussed the workday, each of them shared how the memories in the living room of warm family interaction had affected their lives. None of them could bring themselves to tear down the room that had so many pleasant memories for them.

How pleasant is our home? I think of the kitchen or dining room where families have meals together. I can tell you this—mealtime with your family is sacred. This is a time to affirm one another. All that you say and do in your home molds the life of a child. The consequences of your interactions build memories.

I recently had a client ask me to prepare his tax return separate from his wife. To my surprise, he told me they had been separated for four years and were going through a divorce. They were longtime clients, and I thought their boys were grown and gone from the home. I prepared his return and called him. He then decided to change it, as his two boys were living with him again and he wanted to claim them. I asked about their ages, and he told me they were twenty-four and twenty-eight. I told him he could only claim them if their income was below the personal exemption amount. I gave him the amount, and he said he doubted that either of them worked that much during the year. They did not attend college that year either.

I wonder how much time he invested in the lives of these boys when they were growing up. I doubt he paid much attention to them because even now he was not sure what they were doing. Even though they had lived in the same house for more than two decades, he seemed to be absent from their lives. His lack of knowledge about their work and activities when they live in the same house indicates a lack of communication. This pattern began when these boys were young. Had he bonded with his sons and spent time with them, they might have turned out to be responsible adults. Generally, parents who spend time with their children will see them mature into responsible adults.

Years ago, our family took a one-week summer vacation to Palm Desert, California. This is the hottest time of the year for that area. We used the hot season to our advantage. We rented a house that had a pool and spa. My wife sewed, the children played in the pool, and I lounged poolside, reading. In the afternoon, we all swam together. At night, we got ready and went into town for dinner and sightseeing. Every morning, my wife and I got up just at dawn and took a walk to a small cluster of stores about a mile away. We liked to stop at a real-estate storefront office to look at a cartoon they had in the window. It had a profound message that was a good reminder to us to work together as parents. The first frame showed two mules tied together with a rope and they were pulling away from each other in opposite directions as they each sought out a stack of hay on opposite ends from each other. As you faced the frame, one was pulling to the right and the other was pulling to the left, their backs to each other. The next frame shows both eating from the same stack of hay on the right. They figured out they could not have both stacks at the same time and had to settle for something that allowed them to eat.

A successful marriage depends on a husband and wife working together rather than pulling away from each other. During World War II, in the Pacific, Lt. Col. Evans F. Carlson, of Marine Corps Raiders fame, used the motivational term *gung-ho* to inspire his men. He served in China and learned this phrase from the Chinese military. It means “work together.”

In today’s meaning, if a married couple is gung-ho, it means they are working together and sold out for each other in total dedication. We need more couples to catch the gung-ho spirit toward each other and work together on their marriage and family issues. Guys, if you are gung-ho for your wife, let her know it by doing something kind for her unexpectedly.

Some families are defeated from working together because of addictions and other dysfunctional behaviors. These kinds of behaviors destroy families and leave a lasting impact on their children. I come from a line of alcoholics from father to father. My dad's father was an alcoholic. His father was from the Cole clan who left Virginia, migrated to Missouri, and founded Cole County in Missouri. My dad's father then migrated to Kentucky.

My grandfather's nephew told me that his father and my grandfather, brothers, were run out of Kentucky for bootlegging. Both fled to Ohio and stayed there. I only saw my grandfather sober once, and it was when he visited us in California. I was six years old. The two other times I saw him were in Ohio, and he was drunk both times. He sat on his porch, chewed tobacco, and drank from a flask. When his Social Security check came, he got on his bicycle and wobbled down the road to the

Red Parrot bar a few blocks from his home in Ravenna, Ohio. He was a regular there.

Unfortunately, he wasted his life as a drunkard and never was able to develop a relationship with God. This placed a heavy responsibility on my grandmother Lizzie. They had fifteen children. Only eight of them survived to adulthood. Some of this was in part due to my grandfather's inattention to the medical needs of his children. My grandmother took care of things that were his responsibility. Lizzie kept the remaining family together through loyal, steadfast, hardworking perseverance. He missed a wonderful life that the Lord had laid out for him.

In my family, alcoholism stopped after my father. I wish my grandfather could have read Psalm 139:17 when he was a young man. In this Psalm, King David says, "How precious also are thy thoughts unto me, O God! how great is the sum of them!" He would have realized the attributes of God and His plan for life.

When you pass the baton, it is for good things. The most important baton to pass on to your children is a saving knowledge of Jesus Christ as their savior. If they understand, accept salvation, and know Him, then you have passed on the baton. Other things should then fall into place, such as a strong work ethic, responsibility, good citizenship, and a caring attitude toward others. The things you say and do influence the generations following you. Your children and grandchildren watch what you do. They hear what you say. They try to copy you.

Oral history has been very important over the generations. In Boaz's time, it was how important events were communicated to each successive generation. Boaz and Ruth probably told Obed many stories about themselves and their ancestors. Obed in turn communicated these important events to his children, and the stories would continue to succeeding generations.

In Psalm 19 David records how God reveals Himself and His glory to us. As a young man, David developed a heart for the things of the Lord. No doubt Boaz had an influence on him through Obed and Jesse. David ended the Psalm in verse fourteen with "Let the words of my mouth and the meditation of my heart, be acceptable in thy sight, O Lord, my strength and my Redeemer."

David did not always follow the ways of the Lord, but he knew better.

Whom are you influencing today? You have a baton—in fact, you have several of them—to pass on to your descendants and others. You may never know your impact on a child in Sunday school or a neighbor kid. In your home and community, you can make a difference in the life of a child.

When our children were young, we sat down with each one of them and made a special flag named after them. On a special day, we hung the flag in front of our house and named the day after the child the flag represented. My wife was a stay-at-home mom, so she was able to devote considerable time to our children. I remember one evening coming home from work and seeing my wife with traces of military camouflage on her face. I asked her about it, and she said that when our son came home from school that day, she wanted to spend time with him doing something fun. It was his flag day. He told her he wanted to play army. We had a large piece of property, and our house was on top of a hill. There were trails descending to the horse corrals and our barnyard. It was perfect for playing army.

My wife put on some military gear, painted camouflage on her face, carried a rifle, and went down the trail with our son. They climbed on top of the fort I had built and played army that afternoon. They both had a great time, and this investment of spending time with our son paid off.

Today, more than ever, our influence is critical. Our youth receive conflicting messages about moral values from our culture. They need a stable home environment where a cohesive family provides guidance on life's issues. They also need to attend a Bible-believing church and Sunday school, where important Bible stories are taught.

The Lord has divinely appointed parents to raise their children based on biblical principles. It is evident that Boaz received a lot of instruction and guidance from his parents when he was growing up. He sought out instruction from the Lord. He and Ruth passed on these principles to their descendants. Now the baton is in our hands.

APPENDIX

Study and Discussion Guide

The book of Ruth tells a wonderful story about love, redemption, leadership, and legacy. It is a guide to a strong and lasting marriage. *Leaving A Legacy of Love* fills in a contemporary setting that gives us insight into the daily challenges of marriage and family.

Chapter 1 You Can't Just Live on Love Ruth 1:1 – 2

1. There are times in a marriage when a couple may experience financial difficulty due to job loss, inadequate income, and unexpected expenses. It is important how a couple responds to these challenges. Discuss ways a couple can plan

for these kinds of events and ways they can respond to them when they happen.

2. Prudent financial management is essential to a healthy marriage. Discuss the importance of identifying our wants from needs and how a couple can preserve their financial health.

3. Couples can live with only the barest of necessities and still be content. How is this possible?

4. Is it a good idea to borrow from family members when a couple experiences financial difficulties?

Chapter 2 Losing the Love of Your Life Ruth 1:3 – 6

1. All of us probably know a person who experienced the loss of a loved one. It is not easy and oftentimes prompts deep reflection on life and its meaning. The closer the loved one, and if it was unexpected, the harder it will be to a person than if the loved one were a distant relative and his or her demise was expected. We don't know how a person feels when he or she experiences a loss. Discuss some of the ways to respond to a person who is going through this. Discuss responses that should be avoided.

2. A person who experiences a deep loss may need help during an adjustment period. What are some of the ways we can reach out to a person trying to make a post loss adjustment?

3. Look up some Bible verses that may help us as we minister to others in need. Discuss within the group. The Psalms reflect our vertical relationship with the Lord. The following are Psalms of encouragement:

When a person feels abandoned

Psalm 10

When a person's world seems to be falling apart

Psalm 46

When a person is afraid

Psalm 23 and 91

When a person feels like God has forgotten him or her Psalm 139

When a person is tempted to lose faith in God Psalm 62

When a person has suffered a loss, we need to be careful about the timing of giving them Bible verses. We need to have God affirming verses in our heart, so we know how to respond if asked. A person in a delicate situation may ask you for comforting words from the Lord. Having gained his or her request, it may be appropriate to read or quote scripture. Sometimes our just being there and saying nothing is all that is needed.

4. Sometimes people only wish someone well. Other times people are more committed and do someone well. A committed person who helps

someone does it privately. Discuss ways we can help others who have suffered a loss and are in need.

Chapter 3 Journey Home Ruth 1:7 – 22

1. You may know people who moved far away from their hometown, lived in their new

surroundings for several years, and then later were prompted by thoughts of how great the past was, and returned to their hometown. This usually occurs when circumstances change for the worse and they romanticize about their youth. Sometimes it is related to retirement. They want to retire to the town of their youth. How do we know when the Lord wants us to move to another location? How can we discern His will? What should we consider about our family?

2. In this move Naomi had a loyal companion, Ruth. Ruth did not question her motive for moving back to Bethlehem. Ruth wanted to be with her. Married couples need to foster a relationship where they can make major decisions together. It is important they agree on making a move. Discuss the main points to consider in making a move to another community.

3. Has God ever moved you to something new and different and you did not realize why at the time, but it all made sense later?

4. Prayer takes center stage in all that we do. God orchestrated Naomi's move with Ruth as her companion. Have you seen or read about other examples where people prayed, and God orchestrated a move to a strange land? Sometimes God commands a person to move. (Read Genesis 12:1).

1. Boaz was a true manager and leader. He owned his own business and looked out for his employees. What are some of the things he did to earn their respect?

2. What are the qualities we see in Boaz?

3. Ruth was a caring person who initiated helping Naomi. What are some of the things she did to help her?

4. What are the qualities we see in Ruth?

Chapter 5 A Man and His Role Ruth 2:8 – 23

1. Boaz set an example of a take charge person when he was told of Ruth and her status. What did he do to help Ruth and Naomi?

2. Part of the definition of love for a man is to provide for and protect his wife. What does this mean?

3. What did Boaz do to provide for and protect Ruth?

4. Are young men today being prepared for marriage responsibilities? How can parents prepare boys for their God given role in adulthood?

Chapter 6 A Man Proves His Worth Ruth 3:1 – 18

1. What are the steps Boaz took when he was told of his redeemer status?

2. Boaz followed through on his responsibilities. Discuss how important this is for a man in a marriage.

3. Boaz looked at marriage as a life-long commitment. What needs to be done in a marriage to make sure it is not just a marriage of convenience that can be broken at any time?

4. What should a person look for in a potential lifelong partner?

Chapter 7 Take Responsibility

Ruth 4:1 – 12

1. Boaz followed through on his responsibility to become Ruth's kinsman- redeemer. One of the problems in marriage is men not taking the initiative to help-out in the home and to become

the spiritual leader. Discuss what it takes to help men become aware of their responsibilities.

2. How can we discern who to marry?

3. What are the responsibilities in a marriage?

4. What are the expectations in a marriage?

Chapter 8 A Lifetime Journey Ruth 4:13 – 17

1. Why are grandparents important in a family structure?

2. How long should a marriage partner hold onto bitterness and resentment?

3. Is it a good idea to resolve all issues before turning the lights out for the night?

4. How can couples continue the spark of their love for one another?

Chapter 9 Family Legacy Ruth 4:18 – 22

1. We oftentimes see the result of our parenting in the life of our adult children. There are exceptions to this as some parents do a great job of raising their children only to see them fall prey to our corrupt culture. Discuss your vision for

your descendants and what it will take in your home to accomplish this.

2. What can we do in our home to make it as pleasant as possible?

3. Are we spending our time on family rather than things that will disappear in a year or two?

4. How often do we pray for our descendants?

Chapter 10 Called for His Purpose Joshua 2:1 – 21, 6:22 – 23

1. Some people reflect on life with regret for things they have done wrong or things they should have done. We all have worth. God takes unlikely people and has them do great things for Him. Discuss ways we can see the potential in our spouse and help him or her utilize God given talents.

2. In God's providence he orchestrated Rahab helping the Israelites and becoming Boaz' mother. Discuss the role of prayer in petitioning the Lord to orchestrate His will.

3. If married, how can we encourage our spouse today?

4. How do we build fond memories?

Chapter 11 A Strong Marriage

Ephesians 5:33 and Titus 2:2 – 6

Building a strong marriage to withstand the stress and adversity of life requires dedication to godly principles. What are your suggestions for the following:

1. Discuss suggestions for the husband.

2. Discuss suggestions for the wife.

3. Discuss suggestions for both as a couple.

4. Are there any other considerations that would be helpful to a marriage?

Chapter 12 Passing the Baton

Deuteronomy 11:18 - 20

1. What are some of the ways we can remember to pray for our descendants?

2. How can we influence our descendants as our family grows?

3. Discuss the importance of telling family stories of faith to your children.

4. What would you like your grandchildren and beyond to say about you?

www.ingramcontent.com/pod-product-compliance
Lightning Source LLC
LaVergne TN
LVHW091209150826
845672LV00005B/1294

* 9 7 9 8 3 5 8 9 8 3 4 1 0 *